Integrating
ENVIRONMENTAL
PRINT Across the Curriculum, PreK-3

Making Literacy Instruction Meaningful

LYNN KIRKLAND
JERRY ALDRIDGE
PATRICIA KUBY

CORWIN PRESS
A SAGE Publications Company
Thousand Oaks, CA 91320

For information:

Corwin Press
A Sage Publications Company
2455 Teller Road
Thousand Oaks, California 91320
www.corwinpress.com

Sage Publications Ltd.
1 Oliver's Yard
55 City Road
London EC1Y 1SP
United Kingdom

Sage Publications India Pvt. Ltd.
B-42, Panchsheel Enclave
Post Box 4109
New Delhi 110 017 India

Printed in the United States of America.

Library of Congress Cataloging-in-Publication Data

Kirkland, Lynn.
Integrating environmental print across the curriculum, preK-3 : making literacy instruction meaningful / Lynn Kirkland, Jerry Aldridge, Patricia Kuby.
    p. cm.
Includes bibliographical references and index.
ISBN-13: 978-1-4129-3757-3 (cloth)
ISBN-13: 978-1-4129-3758-0 (pbk.)
  1. Language arts (Early childhood) 2. Early childhood education—Activity programs. 3. Interdisciplinary approach in education. I. Aldridge, Jerry. II. Kuby, Patricia. III. Title.

LB1139.5.L35K57 2007
372.6—dc22

                                                    2006030724

This book is printed on acid-free paper.

06 07 08 09 10 10 9 8 7 6 5 4 3 2 1

Acquisitions Editor:	Stacy Wagner
Editorial Assistant:	Joanna Coelho
Production Editor:	Jenn Reese
Copy Editor:	Cheryl Duksta
Typesetter:	C&M Digitals (P) Ltd.
Proofreader:	Victoria Reed-Castro
Cover Designer:	Monique Hahn
Interior Design	Good Neighbor Press, Inc.

Contents

Acknowledgments

This book is the result of the inspiration and efforts of many individuals beyond the authors. We would like to thank the following people: Dr. Robert J. Canady deserves much credit for being the first to introduce us to environmental print. The work he began with his students will continue for centuries to come. The research of Dr. Yetta Goodman in the area of environmental print has also inspired much of our research and writing. Further, many of our students and former students, especially classroom teachers, have contributed greatly to our knowledge and experience in environmental print. One student in particular, Leigh Ann Summerford, deserves special mention. Finally, we would like to dedicate this book to our families.

Corwin Press would like to thank the following peer reviewers for their editorial insight and guidance:

Devin Caldwell
Kindergarten Teacher
Grissom Elementary School
Tulsa, OK

Sarah Farrell
Family Literacy Coordinator
Shining Stars Preschool
Rio Rancho, NM

Yetta M. Goodman
Regents Professor Emerita
Department of Language, Reading and Culture
University of Arizona

Myae Han
Assistant Professor
Department of Individual and Family Studies
University of Delaware

Trudy Henry
Kindergarten Teacher
Chinooks Edge School Division
Benalto, Alberta, Canada

Karen Jurgensen
Title I Teacher
Flour Bluff Primary School
Corpus Christi, TX

About the Authors

Lynn Kirkland, EdD, is associate professor of early childhood education at the University of Alabama at Birmingham. During the summers, she directs the UAB Children's Creative Learning Center, a 6-week summer enrichment program for children. She has published numerous articles on early childhood and literacy development. She is coauthor of the book *Connectors: Content Area Studies in Early Childhood,* published by the Association for Childhood Education International.

Jerry Aldridge, EdD, is professor of curriculum and instruction and coordinator of the doctoral program in early childhood education at the University of Alabama at Birmingham. He is a former president of the U.S. chapter of the World Organization for Early Childhood Education (OMEP) and is currently on the publications committee of the Association for Childhood Education International. He has published numerous articles in early childhood, literacy, and special education.

Patricia Kuby, PhD, is associate professor and chair of early childhood education at Athens State University in Alabama. She learned to appreciate the importance of environmental print as her children read signs and logos while traveling on family car trips. Her three children are now all educators. Patricia is past president of the Alabama Association for the Education of Young Children. She has published numerous articles on literacy development and early childhood.

Introduction

There are important ways to tap into what a child already knows and use this to jump-start the literacy process.

Helping children become good readers and writers is no easy task—or is it? While learning to read and write takes time, there are important ways to tap into what a child already knows and use this to jump-start the literacy process. One of these important ways is through environmental print. Environmental print is defined "as print found in the natural environment of the child. This would include logos, labels, road signs, billboards, and other print found in the child's immediate ecology" (Kirkland, Aldridge, & Kuby, 1991, p. 219).

We have been researching and writing about environmental print for almost 2 decades now. In 1991, we self-published an early version of the book you now hold in your hands. Back then, the educational climate was vastly different, but the need for quality literacy resources for teachers was just as critical. We wrote the book using our own experiences of what worked, combined with research that was current at the time. Research conducted by others since then has emphasized the importance of early instruction in print knowledge and print awareness in creating successful readers. We've been heartened by these findings, which convinced us that our work is just as relevant as before—if not more so—given the current emphasis on making every child a reader.

 ## Findings of the National Reading Panel

In 2000, the National Reading Panel released its report *Teaching Children to Read,* which heavily influenced the No Child Left Behind (NCLB) legislation, signed into law in early 2002. To assist schools in meeting the reading requirements of NCLB, the federal government added two new initiatives as part of the legislation: the Early Reading First initiative for children ages 3–5 years and the Reading First initiative for children in kindergarten through third grade. Schools receiving Early Reading First grants, Reading First grants, or both, are responsible for achieving marked development in the following areas:

Early Reading First	Reading First
Oral language (vocabulary, expressive language, listening comprehension)	Phonemic awareness
Phonological awareness (rhyming, blending, segmenting)	Phonics
Print awareness	Vocabulary
Alphabetic knowledge	Fluency
	Comprehension

Based on the findings of the National Reading Panel report, however, even schools that do not receive federal grants for these programs still strive to develop children's abilities in these areas, so children can become successful readers. At the same time, teachers recognize that learning in the early years should be a joyous experience and are searching for effective instructional practices that are both academically sound and developmentally appropriate (Copple & Bredekamp, 2005).

Making Meaningful Connections With Environmental Print

Considering the research pointing toward the critical skills young readers need to be successful, let's turn to three specific questions:

1. Why use environmental print?

2. How can I use environmental print in my classroom?

3. What is the value of environmental print?

Why Use Environmental Print?

Environmental print is important to use throughout the curriculum for a number of reasons, including these few:

Children see environmental print is everywhere. Even children who are not read to often see print in their natural environments (Prior & Gerard, 2004).

Children can use the print they see in the environment to help them learn. Children are not blank slates. They are active constructors of knowledge. Children try to make sense out of what they see in their environment (Christie, Enz, Gerard, & Prior, 2002).

Children can make the transition from home to school much easier when they see something familiar (such as environmental print) in the classroom (Kirkland et al., 1991). Teachers who incorporate an environmental print alphabet in their classroom allow children to feel at home with logos they have seen in their neighborhood (e.g., logos for Kentucky Fried Chicken, Kmart, McDonald's). Children are more likely to learn the alphabet when it is associated with something familiar (Copple & Bredekamp, 2005).

Children can actively participate by bringing in print from the environment and sharing it with others. Most teachers have a sharing time each day. This sharing time may be called circle time, daily news, or planning time, among other names. Children can be encouraged to bring in logos from their neighborhood and place them in a large environmental print box. At sharing time, the children can discuss all of the logos brought in that day and the experiences they have had with each. A student might say, "My grandma took me to Pizza Hut last night." Another might add, "My cousins went with me and my mom to Toys-R-Us, and we bought a board game." The teacher or a student can serve as a scribe and write the experiences on an overhead, the chalkboard, or a chart.

So why is this important? When children first begin to read, they need to go from the familiar to the unfamiliar, from the known to the unknown (Vygotsky, 1978). Having children share environmental print items they are familiar with gives them ownership of their learning. This ownership empowers them. The children share their experiences, and these experiences, in turn, have a profound effect on children's literacy development.

Environmental print breaks through curricular boundaries and supports an integrated curriculum (Kirkland et al., 1991). Many early childhood classrooms use integrated teaching or thematic units. However, it is sometimes hard to authentically incorporate all of the areas of the curriculum into these units. Environmental print naturally breaks through curriculum boundaries and serves as a foundation for literacy activities. Newspapers and catalogs serve as rich material for mathematics—for example, they can be used to make shopping lists. Transportation schedules add a rich dimension to social studies, and using food labels and recipes provides a meaningful source for science activities. Books that use environmental print are listed in Resource A.

---

*Environmental print is one of the most natural
ways to build an integrated curriculum.
(Prior & Gerard, 2004)*

How Can I Use Environmental Print in My Classroom?

We have come a long way in a short time in learning how to use environmental print. When we first started using it in our classrooms, we became fat, irritable, and exhausted! How did that happen? Well, we drove all over town, eating junk food, collecting garbage, and making games for our classrooms (often staying up half the night). While we intuitively knew environmental print would be good for our students, we did not yet know how to implement it. Although this was a start, it had little value for our students because the environmental print had not come from them.

Now we know better. Students have to have shared ownership in the program. They must bring in the environmental print, discuss it, classify it, use it, make games with it, and be the primary participants in the process. Based on what we learned, we make the following recommendations on how you can use environmental print.

Inform and involve parents and families. Parents and families will wonder what you are doing if they are not included as important participants in environmental print. To achieve parents' active participation, first meet with parents or guardians. Explain that their children will be asked to bring in print they have already experienced. Parents also need to be encouraged to point out labels and signs and encourage their children to seek them out in their immediate surroundings. A sample letter to parents, explaining how to use environmental print, is included in Appendix B.

Get the children involved immediately. At the beginning of the school year, children should be encouraged to bring in print. Give them examples of where it can be found: restaurants, convenience stores, can or box labels, and billboards. Then tell them to place what they bring to class in the environmental print box. Not only will they discuss the print at share time, but students also will be provided the opportunity to use the environmental print to classify in science, make games and books in math and literacy, invent through creative arts, and develop motor skills through active, hands-on learning.

Have the students help develop the program. Shared involvement is essential. Teachers and children should work together to create the environmental print program by sharing ideas and interests. This book is designed to help you and your students develop the best environmental print program you can.

What Is the Value of Environmental Print?

Environmental print is only one small piece of the learning process and environment. It is by no means the only piece—but it is an important one. Having an early childhood classroom without using environmental print is like having a jigsaw puzzle with one piece missing. Environmental print is important for many reasons. A few are listed in this section.

Having an early childhood classroom without using environmental print is like having a jigsaw puzzle with one piece missing.

Environmental print uses the prior knowledge of the students. We now know that for students to learn at their best we must incorporate, as much as possible, their prior experiences and knowledge into the curriculum (Copple & Bredekamp, 2005).

Environmental print provides an authentic, legitimate purpose for learning. Students at every grade level often fail to see the value of what they are learning or its relationship to the real world. Text doesn't get any more "real world" than environmental print. Using the knowledge children bring to school with them sets the stage for further learning (Prior & Gerard, 2004).

Environmental print has both constructive and instructive value. Children construct their own knowledge about print by interacting with logos and sharing them with others. However, children have great difficulty recognizing these logos when they are typed on paper or handwritten on the chalkboard, overhead, or paper. This situation brings about the instructive value of environmental print. Teachers can serve as important models by writing the names of products children bring into the classroom. This way, children can make the transition from logos to standard print. Children are less likely to construct manuscript versions of logos without the teacher's modeling (Prior, 2004).

Environmental print can be used to teach all of the skills that the National Reading Panel (2000) has determined to be the best predictors of how children learn to read. Environmental print can be used to develop oral language fluency, phonological awareness, print awareness, and alphabetic knowledge. Through storytelling and daily news activities, environmental print is a great vehicle for oral language development. Associating the sounds of language with environmental print helps make phonological awareness easier. Awareness of print can also be achieved by assisting children in distinguishing the print found in the environment from supporting background material. And, finally, learning the alphabet is more easily achieved through meaningful experiences using environmental print.

As you'll see, the environmental print activities presented in this book are fun, engaging, and research supported to help you bring about early literacy in all areas of the curriculum. We've specifically pointed out the early literacy skills that each activity helps to develop, while ensuring that learning to read can and should be an enjoyable experience.

We close this introductory chapter by looking at the physical environment of the classroom and how environmental print can be used to enhance it. The following classroom is a print-rich environment, using what the students have brought to it. The literacy center (in particular) presents children with opportunities for experimentation with language as a whole. Whole texts from literature, newspapers, and advertisements—in children's own language as well as the language of learning—are used for language experience charts, pocket charts, and games. Children "play" with language, moving from whole to part. They start with whole texts, move to parts, and then finally move to letters. Alphabet books, word books, and dictionaries are kept in the literacy center as resources for the children when needed. (Note: Some teachers choose to have a literacy center separate from their library.

Others use the classroom library as a literacy center.) Children make their own books, dictionaries, and games. A storage box or large can is placed in the center and used to keep environmental print labels and logos brought in by the children. Scissors, tape, and glue are readily available to encourage independent work.

Additional ideas for incorporating environmental print in other areas of the classroom and curriculum are detailed in this book. We hope you will enjoy your journey into integrating the curriculum through environmental print. All students can benefit from a jump-start, and a familiar, print-rich environment gets them well on their way to becoming readers.

CHAPTER ONE

What We Know About Environmental Print and Young Children

From Theory and Research to Practice

The strategies, activities, and games offered in this book are not just cute ideas. They represent what we have learned from a growing body of research about how children learn to read and write with the help of logos, labels, road signs, billboards, and other print found in their natural environment. This chapter is divided into three sections. The first section describes the conceptual framework for environmental print. The second part explains what researchers have discovered about children and environmental print. Finally, the third piece describes appropriate ways to use environmental print.

The Conceptual Framework for Using Environmental Print

The 2nd week of the school year has just begun, and Michelle's principal drops by for a short visit. As Beth, the principal, moves slowly throughout the room, she notices some children sorting logos, others are making books using cereal boxes, while others are in a restaurant center playing customers, waiter, and clerk. Beth seems amused but is not sure what is going on or why. She politely asks Michelle to explain. Michelle is quick to point out that some of the children are engaged in environmental print games and activities. While Michelle seems confident in telling what is happening, she is less sure about the second important question that Beth asks: "Why are the children doing this?" Though we don't expect Michelle to launch into the numerous research studies that have been conducted on the efficacy of environmental print, we hope she will be able to tell her principal a bit about the theories that underlie its use and some key findings that support it.

Constructivism and Contextualism

Environmental print is based on the theories of constructivism and developmental contextualism, as well as what we know about early literacy. While there are many "brands" of constructivism, Piaget is most recognized for his general scientific theory about how children construct knowledge (Goretta, 1977; Kamii, 1991; Piaget, 1970). Although he did not propose a specific theory about reading and writing (Kamii, 1991), Piaget's theory of how children construct knowledge provided a much broader framework that allows individuals to understand any process of acquiring knowledge (Ferreiro & Teberosky, 1982). Simply put, children construct knowledge from the inside out by interacting with their environment. This is true for literacy in general and for environmental print more specifically.

Children construct knowledge from the inside out by interacting with their environment.

Vygotsky (1978) also recognized the importance of children's construction of knowledge but took a more contextual view. Vygotsky created a theory that allowed for both the natural line that emerges from within the child and the social-historical line that influences the child from without. One of Vygotsky's greatest contributions was his idea of the zone of proximal development. Each child has a *zone of proximal development*, defined as the distance between the child's actual developmental level, as determined by the child's independent problem-solving ability, and the level of potential development, as determined through problem solving with adult guidance or peer collaboration. Since literacy is specific to each language and culture, a young child needs some assistance in making sense of environmental print from a more able peer or teacher.

Bronfenbrenner (1977, 1986) believed that children are influenced by multiple contexts in which there are reciprocal interactions between children and their environments. Children are affected by face-to-face interactions, such as those that occur at home or school. However, children are also influenced by their parents' or guardians' workplace and the social, historical, political, and economic realities of the times. The day-to-day context of children is especially important in using environmental print to plan and implement an integrated curriculum to meet children's needs.

What We Know About Early Literacy

The effective use of environmental print has also developed from what we have learned about early literacy. Ferreiro and Teberosky (1982) studied the literacy knowledge of first-grade children before instruction in reading began and later at various times during the school year. They found that

Barone – U of Nevada, Reno
Taylor – teacher consultant – Title I schools – Reno/Sparks areas in NV

Who handles the IRA account? Do we have one? We should! Diane Barone is very well known and well-respected at IRA. Headquarters in Delaware.

Up sell with:
Reading First and Beyond (Barone is very well known among RF people)
Reading and Language Arts Worksheets Don't Grow Dendrites
Differentiated Assessment Strategies

Good classroom assessments—differentiated assessments— better prepare students for standardized tests. This book addresses:
Writing assessments (essay writing)
Reading assessments (measure all areas of Reading First)
Listening and speaking assessments (interviews, presentations)
Visual assessments (digital, internet, video/animation, maps, tables, flowcharts)

Key words:
Formative assessments
Rubrics
Checklists
High-stakes tests
SAT

Kirkland, Aldridge, Kuby – University of Alabama, Birmingham

Audience:
Schools receiving Early Reading First and Reading First grants
Title I directors

Up sell with:
Reading First and Beyond (Barone is very well known among RF people)
Reading and Language Arts Worksheets Don't Grow Dendrites

Barone – U of Nevada, Reno
Taylor – teacher consultant – Title I schools – Reno/Sparks areas in NV

Who handles the IRA account? Do we have one? We should! Diane Barone is very well known and well-respected at IRA. Headquarters in Delaware.

<u>Up sell with</u>:
Reading First and Beyond (Barone is very well known among RF people)
Reading and Language Arts Worksheets Don't Grow Dendrites
Differentiated Assessment Strategies

Good classroom assessments—differentiated assessments— better prepare students for standardized tests. This book addresses:
Writing assessments (essay writing)
Reading assessments (measure all areas of Reading First)
Listening and speaking assessments (interviews, presentations)
Visual assessments (digital, internet, video/animation, maps, tables, flowcharts)

Key words:
Formative assessments
Rubrics
Checklists
High-stakes tests
SAT

Kirkland, Aldridge, Kuby – University of Alabama, Birmingham

Audience:
Schools receiving Early Reading First and Reading First grants
Title I directors

<u>Up sell with</u>:
Reading First and Beyond (Barone is very well known among RF people)
Reading and Language Arts Worksheets Don't Grow Dendrites

children's learning processes may take paths unsuspected by the teacher. Even the children with limited exposure to print had accumulated knowledge about print before they came to school.

To further explore the influence of the environment and what children know about print at different ages, Ferreiro and Teberosky (1982) undertook another study of children from lower- and middle-class backgrounds. The middle-class children were 4 and 5 years of age and attended private kindergartens or preschools. The lower-class 4- and 5-year-olds attended kindergarten or preschools attached to public schools. After analyzing their data, Ferreiro and Teberosky attempted to explain the developmental processes of children learning to read and write and to offer their interpretations and implications for instruction. They found that young children progress through various hypotheses about written language until they develop ideas similar to those of older children. It was their observation that children are not passive learners of language but active participants in the language of their environment.

*Even children with limited exposure to print
accumulate knowledge about print
before they come to school.*

Yetta Goodman (1984b), through years of study on how children construct literacy, also realized that children's inventions and approximations about literacy in a society full of print begin long before the child comes to school. Goodman recognized the importance of social context and a developmental view of learning. She also hypothesized that children develop ideas about literacy just as they develop ideas in other areas of learning. Children actively construct their notions concerning literacy through their participation in a literate society.

More recently, Piper (2003) synthesized the research on early language and literacy development and found six factors related to preschool learning that are of particular importance when children enter school:

1. Children's readiness varies greatly.

2. Children have a large say in what they will and will not learn.

3. Play is important to children's language and literacy learning and development.

4. Parents are facilitators, not instructors.

5. Social interaction is central to children's language and literacy learning.

6. In fact, language learning is best achieved through social interaction.

Environmental print can easily address these six factors related to preschool learning. We have found that environmental print can be used to accommodate different levels of readiness, encourage literacy play, and promote social interaction necessary for literacy learning.

Research on Environmental Print

A joint literacy statement published by six professional national education organizations (Schickedanz, 1986) included a list of what young children already know before they come to school. The professional organizations agreed that many children are reading environmental print, such as road signs, grocery labels, and fast-food signs, before they come to school (Kuby, Goodstadt-Killoran, Aldridge, & Kirkland, 1999).

Reading environmental print is something children often engage in before reading print in books (Aldridge & Rust, 1987; Letchman, Finn, & Aldridge, 1991; McGee, 1986; Miller, 1998; Prior & Gerard, 2004; Wepner, 1985). Marie Clay (1993) found that children explore the details of print in their environment—on signs, on cereal packages, and in television advertisements. They develop concepts about print in their environment and about books. Consequently, more advanced concepts emerge out of children's earlier understandings. This leads to the formation of primitive hypotheses about letters, words, or messages they see.

Children explore the details of print in their environment—on signs, on cereal packages, and in television advertisements.

Jump-Starting the Literacy Process

Clay (1993) wrote about the widely held belief that school is easier for children who had a rich preschool literacy experience than for those who had few such opportunities for learning. She believed that all children are ready to learn something but will start at different places. When children enter school, it is the teacher's responsibility to find out where they are developmentally—what they know and can do—and to build on that foundation, whether it is rich or meager. Clay thought that each child must be allowed to start with what he or she already knows and use that knowledge to support what has to be learned next. Most children already know some environmental print when they enter school.

Adams (1990) suggested that children who grow up in a print-rich environment seem to learn that print is different from other kinds of visual patterns in their environment. They also learn that print is print across any variety of physical media. Children notice that print is all around them and that it forms different categories, such as books, newspapers, lists, and price tags. It appears on signs, boxes, television, or fabric. Soon, children notice that print is used by adults in different ways. Children quickly realize that print symbolizes language and holds information—for example, the TV schedule tells them whether there is anything interesting on television. They also learn that print can be produced by anyone.

Children quickly realize that print symbolizes language and holds information.

From major research on early literacy development conducted with Spanish-speaking children in Mexico and Argentina (Ferreiro & Teberosky, 1982), Yetta Goodman (1986) concluded "that the differences in language did not constitute a barrier to the application of basic ideas in a field so language dependent as literacy" (p. 12). Lee's (1989) research on emergent literacy of Mandarin-speaking children in Taiwan supported Goodman's conclusions. Lee found that children in Taiwan were aware of environmental print, just as American children were, even before they received formal reading and writing instruction. These Taiwanese children also relied on contextual clues, with young children (3-year-olds) being less able than older children to read environmental print.

Case Studies on Early Literacy Development

Harste, Burke, and Woodward (1982) attempted to explain further the process of growing print awareness in children by having 4-year-olds perform several tasks, the first of which involved environmental print. The authors made the following conclusions at the end of their research:

- Preschool children discover much about print prior to formal language instruction.

- Formal instruction programs often assume that young children know little of anything about print.

- Teachers should begin formal language instruction by building on the many language strategies that children have already developed on their own.

- Teachers need to assist children in discovering the predictability of written language in a variety of real-world, whole language contexts.

Woodward, Harste, and Burke (1984) affirmed that children's experiences in reading signs and logos are valuable. The authors observed and interacted with children to discover how they deliberated about logos. Their findings were that the children's responses concerning the logos were the direct outcome of their previous experiences.

Bissex (1980) observed her son Paul learning to read and write. The first two words he learned to read were his name and the word "Exit," in the context of a green sign on the side of the road.

Laminack (1991) studied his son Zachary's reactions to many different print forms beginning at 15 months of age.

Miller (1996, 1998) studied her daughter Katie from 3 to 5 years of age and found that she explored environmental print on a daily basis, including junk mail and the newspaper.

Print Knowledge

Yetta Goodman (1984a) noted that even those children whose standardized tests predicted failure in reading demonstrated that they had knowledge about written language. They knew that the print in books and on other objects in the environment communicated written language messages. They understood the meaning of the sign that says "stop," even though sometimes they referred to the word as "don't go" or "brake car" before they learned the words "stop." In another study, Goodman (1980) found that children learn about reading and writing as they participate in environmental print activities.

Contextual Clues

Ylisto (1967) believed that children proceed through a process of learning to read environmental print in five identifiable steps:

1. Seeing a *photograph* of a symbol in its natural setting
2. Seeing a *drawing* of the symbol in its natural setting
3. Seeing the *symbol* printed *in isolation*
4. Seeing the *symbol* printed *in a sentence*
5. Seeing the *symbol* printed *in story context*

In early studies of environmental print conducted by Ylisto (1967) and others (Cloer, Aldridge, & Dean, 1981/1982), the authors concluded that many children learning to read environmental print were unable to successfully read symbols in the later stages when they were presented without contextual clues. However, a more recent study by Kuby, Aldridge, and Snyder (1994) found that kindergarten children increased their noncontextual word recognition when their teachers took time during environmental print instruction to write the words of the logos in manuscript form. As a result, these students were better able to make the transition from logos in context to logos written in manuscript to logos embedded in a sentence and to logos typed.

Noncontextual word recognition increases when teachers take the time to write the words of logos in manuscript form.

Attitudes Toward Reading

Wepner's (1985) study of 3.5- and 4.5-year-olds from middle-class homes found that those who used logo books for 15 to 20 minutes per week with a researcher were able to identify more logos than others in a control group that did not use the logo books, were more positive about their ability to learn to read than those in the control group, and were more aware of print in their environment than those in the control group. They also displayed more confidence and competence in reading words after the study concluded.

By using print in children's natural surroundings, children learn to recognize logos in and out of context (Wepner, 1985). Wepner also believed that linking logos of places and things with important people in the children's lives helped them develop competence and self-esteem. Children who experience success will approach reading eagerly instead of with fear.

Adult Intervention and Supervision

Several studies (Kuby & Aldridge, 1997; Neuman & Roskos, 1993; Vukelich, 1994) focused on the effects of adult intervention or supervision, or both, using environmental print in learning centers or play episodes with young children. Vukelich analyzed the influence of interactions with environmental print in a literacy play setting among 56 kindergarten children and adult partners. Results indicated that print-enriched play with an adult offered numerous opportunities for children to associate meaning with print.

Neuman and Roskos (1993) used eight Head Start classrooms with 177 children (98% African American; 2% Hispanic) to create three groups exposed to three conditions:

1. A literacy-enriched, generic, office play setting, with an adult encouraged to give active assistance to children's literacy learning.

2. A literacy-enriched office play setting, with a parent-teacher asked to monitor the children in their literacy play without direct intervention.

3. A nonintervention group.

The children's handling, reading, and writing of environmental and functional print were assessed through direct observations. The office play setting was videotaped weekly to examine children's use of functional items and their interactions with peers and parent-teachers. After completing the intervention, each child was administered environmental print tasks. No differences were found for children's understanding of functional print items used in the study (letter, stamp, calendar, telephone book), but the parent-teacher active engagement with children in the office setting significantly influenced the children's ability to read environmental print and label functional items. This research indicates that the office play setting influences children's environmental-word reading and that the role of the interactive parent-teacher significantly contributes to children's learning of print in these contexts. These findings strongly suggest that the office play setting with the interacting adult assists children in learning more environmental print. This study reported the importance of not only exposure but also interactions with a capable adult in learning environmental print words.

Parent-teacher active engagement with children influences children's abilities to read environmental print and label function items.

Environmental Print and Children With Special Needs

Environmental print instruction has also been investigated for children with special needs. For example, Aldridge and Rust (1987) found that first-grade children in a special education class for children with developmental disabilities benefited from environmental print instruction. Two major findings of this study were that the children were more proactive in seeking out print in their environment, and they saw themselves as readers and writers. In another study with preschool children in an early intervention classroom, Letchman et al. (1991) used environmental print over a 2-year period with 12 children in conjunction with a strong emphasis on letters and sounds. Results showed an increase in the children's attention span, an increase in parental participation with the children and teachers, and active involvement of the children and their families in reading at home.

Using environmental print with children with special needs can increase child attention, parental participation, and active involvement of reading at home.

Environmental Print and No Child Left Behind

As we mentioned in the introduction to this book, the National Reading Panel's report on teaching children to read greatly influenced the No Child Left Behind (NCLB) legislation. According to the U.S. Department of Education (2002), preschool literacy experiences that are based on scientific research should focus on oral language, phonological awareness, print awareness, and alphabetic knowledge. Prior and Gerard (2004) found that environmental print instruction can be used in each of these four areas.

As children proceed from kindergarten through third grade, instruction should focus on phonemic awareness, phonics, vocabulary, fluency, and comprehension (U.S. Department of Education, 2002). Environmental print can be a useful tool in these five salient areas necessary for literacy development (Cummins, 2006). Environmental print is an especially appropriate tool for teaching phonemic awareness (Enz, 2006).

Summary of the Research Findings on Environmental Print

We have learned much about the importance of environmental print through research conducted over the past 40 years. Listed here are nine of the most salient findings:

1. Children learn about reading and writing as they participate in environmental print activities (Kuby & Aldridge, 1997).

2. Environmental print is something children often engage in before reading print in books (Prior & Gerard, 2004).

3. Children's prior knowledge is important to reading development. Most children have environmental print knowledge as part of their prior knowledge (Woodward et al., 1984).

4. Preschool children are especially apt at reading the meaning of the environmental print in context, even if they cannot read the logos in manuscript form (Kuby et al., 1994; Prior & Gerard, 2004).

5. Many children learning to read environmental print are unable to make the transition to environmental print words written in standard manuscript or computer generated. However, adult instruction helps children make this transition (Kuby & Aldridge, 1997).

6. Environmental print is a useful tool in meeting the research-based goals of the National Reading Panel (National Institute of Child Health and Human Development, 2000). For preschool children, these goals include oral language development, phonological awareness, print awareness, and alphabetic knowledge. For children in kindergarten through third grade, these goals include instruction in phonemic awareness, phonics, vocabulary, fluency, and comprehension (Cummins, 2006; Enz, 2006; Prior & Gerard, 2004).

7. Children all over the world who speak languages other than English benefit from environmental print and environmental print instruction (Ferreiro & Teberosky, 1982; Lee, 1989).

8. Environmental print instruction can ease the transition into formal reading by building confidence, competence, and self-esteem (Aldridge & Rust, 1987; Wepner, 1985).

9. Environmental print is effective with children who have special needs. Children in special education who have experienced environmental print instruction are more proactive in seeking out print in their environment than are children with special needs who have not experienced environmental print instruction. Further, children exposed to environmental print see themselves as active readers and writers (Aldridge & Rust, 1987).

 # Appropriate Ways to Use Environmental Print Throughout the Curriculum

From research and our own years of experience with children and environmental print, we make the following recommendations:

1. *Use environmental print to bridge the gap from home to school.* Environmental print is an excellent way to make the home–school connection. Some teachers have students whose second language is English. Some parents may have difficulty speaking, reading, or writing English. Environmental print can be an especially effective tool with these families. For example, most reading experts recommend that parents read to their children every day.

But what about parents who cannot read books? These parents can use environmental print found in the home, neighborhood, and community to work with both the children and the school to become active, contributing members to the classroom community. Further, environmental print is inexpensive and a great means for involving parents, grandparents, and guardians in school participation who might otherwise feel marginalized and remain uninvolved. As we mentioned in the introduction, children are more actively involved in literacy when they can make the home–school connection.

Environmental print is inexpensive and a great means for involving parents, grandparents, and guardians in school participation who might otherwise feel marginalized and remain uninvolved.

2. *Use environmental print to teach letters and words in meaningful context.* Some of the studies cited in this chapter point to children's ability to recognize logos even though they can't recognize the letters or words of the logos when they are typed or written on a chart, chalkboard, or paper. This is where guided instruction comes in. Even a teacher drinking a Coca-Cola soda can point to the can and ask the children, "What does this say?" and then write C-o-k-e on the board and discuss the letters! Of course, there are many more exciting ways presented in this book to use environmental print, but the point we want to make is that this strategy of pointing out letters and words and printing logos on the board (hopefully in stories or some form of meaningful context) is a very simple thing to do.

3. *Use environmental print to teach the areas determined by the National Reading Panel (2000) as necessary for instruction with early readers.* Environmental print can be used to meet the goals of early literacy instruction determined by the National Reading Panel (Enz, 2006). Throughout the book, we suggest activities and strategies that are based on scientific research reported by the National Reading Panel. However, this area is so important we have included a special chapter (Chapter 7) to discuss meeting the goals of the National Reading Panel.

4. *Use environmental print to boost the confidence and self-esteem of all children, especially struggling readers.* As shown in several reported studies, children see themselves as readers and writers and actively seek out print in the environment when environmental print is part of the curriculum. Most of the strategies recommended in this book are appropriate for children who experience early difficulty with reading. Almost all strategies can be used by children with special needs (often with necessary help from a peer or the teacher).

5. *Use environmental print to give students ownership over their learning.* For beginning readers from preschool through first grade, we recommend using an environmental print box or large trashcan for children to place the environmental print they bring to school. At share time, pull out the items the children brought and discuss them. For example, you might ask, "Who brought in the napkin from Pizza Hut? I see Natalie did. Natalie, can you tell us about the experience you had at Pizza Hut?" Then, write this down in the daily news: "Natalie's grandmother took her to Pizza Hut for dinner last night."

Notice that you are helping children make the important transition from the logo to the name in the context of a sentence. However, most children in second grade and higher will have already constructed this on their own. So, for giving older children ownership over their learning using environmental print, we recommend you consult many of the strategies for using environmental print found in this book. Chapter 5, in particular, has numerous strategies for older children.

6. *Use environmental print to integrate curriculum.* Environmental print transcends and has a place in all curricular areas. In the unit "Our Community," environmental print can be used to make maps, determine distance, read signs and logos, sing jingles of local establishments, or learn the history of our area.

7. *Finally, reflect on your use of environmental print and adapt your practice accordingly.* We are always pleased to go into classrooms and see teachers who have used our ideas. We are even more pleased when we see instructors who have invented their own unique ways of using environmental print purposefully. Environmental print, like any other tool, requires a lot of reflection. Remember, it is only one small piece of the curriculum.

The chapters that follow are designed to provide many practical suggestions for using environmental print. Chapter 2 describes language arts activities, while Chapter 3 is concerned with math instruction. Chapter 4 describes ways to use environmental print in health and science. Social studies is the focus of Chapter 5, and art, music, and creative dramatics are highlighted in Chapter 6. Chapter 7 describes important ways to meet the recommendations of the National Reading Panel through the use of environmental print. Finally, the last chapter presents challenges in and opportunities for using environmental print. Environmental print can be used for more than transmission. It has the potential to transform our classrooms, schools, communities, and even the world.

CHAPTER TWO

Language Arts Activities

Research That Informs Language Arts Instruction

As we noted in the introduction, environmental print is just one piece of the early literacy puzzle. However, much has been learned through research about how to effectively use environmental print to help children make the transition from reading logos to reading and writing standard manuscript.

Helping children recognize environmental print is not enough. Several studies have been conducted that show young children have trouble making the transition from the print they see in the environment to the print they see written in standard manuscript or written in books (Cloer et al., 1981/1982; Kuby et al., 1994; Prior & Gerard, 2004; Ylisto, 1967). How can we use this information to encourage literacy development? One way is to demonstrate to children how environmental print can be written and facilitate their writing. A step-by-step approach follows:

1. Have children bring in environmental print with which they have had some experience. For example, say a child named Brittany went with her grandmother to Pizza Hut. Brittany brings in a napkin or cup with a logo of Pizza Hut and places the item in the environmental print box.

2. During circle time or morning planning time, the teacher pulls the environmental print for the day out of the environmental print box and says, "Who brought this?" Brittany explains that she went to Pizza Hut with her grandmother the night before.

3. The teacher models writing on the board, "Brittany went to Pizza Hut with her grandmother last night." The teacher shows the logo on the napkin again and points out that it looks somewhat different from how it appears on the board. The teacher encourages the children to find and highlight the environmental print written in manuscript on the shared writing chart. In shared writing, the teacher and children work together to compose messages and stories with the teacher acting as a scribe (Fountas & Pinnell, 1996). Attention can be called to beginning, middle, or medial sounds in the environmental print. The teacher may also create with the children a shared list of words that have the same phonetic sounds as those in the sentence generated from Brittany's trip to Pizza Hut. Teachers can also compare words from a shared reading text with phonetic sounds found in the environmental print.

4. The teacher continues showing environmental print items that children brought in that day and writes them on the board, in a sentence similar to what was written about Brittany.

5. As a collaborative experience, the children and the teacher post the environmental print on the appropriate alphabet card posted in the classroom. The environmental print can also be placed in an environmental print center for children to post in individual environmental print dictionaries. This example demonstrates one way to connect environmental print to print from texts. The activities presented in this chapter will help teachers to develop and assess early literacy skills while teaching language arts.

Environmental print and language arts go hand in hand. The following activities for using environmental print with language arts are suggested. Use these as is or vary them to meet your own classroom needs:

DAILY NEWS

DAILY NEWS

◆ SUGGESTED GRADE LEVEL

PreK-2

◆ PURPOSE/RATIONALE

- ◆ Provide opportunities to see environmental print in manuscript
- ◆ Increase print awareness skills and alphabetic knowledge by familiarizing children with letters, words, and sentences (Early Reading First goal)
- ◆ Increase oral language skills, particularly vocabulary, expressive language, and listening comprehension (Early Reading First goal)

◆ MATERIALS

- ◆ Labels, logos, symbols, and so forth, brought in by the child
- ◆ Chart tablet or paper for news

◆ PROCEDURE

At some point in the daily news, write with the children about their experiences with the environmental print—for example, "Billy's family ate at McDonald's last night."

◆ VARIATIONS/EXTENSIONS

Diving Deeper Into the Experience

Children can brainstorm things to write about their experience with a particular logo or label. The purpose is to see this print in manuscript or typed in a different context. Using varied contexts for environmental print facilitates word recognition and connections. If the daily news is made into a format to send home with the children, include the children's brainstormed sentences. Individual sentences can be written on sentence strips, cut into individual words, and placed in a plastic bag for children to reconstruct at school or home.

Ensuring Writing Progress

Ensure that children's writing progresses throughout the year by encouraging children to begin to write their own news before the whole group discussion. The introduction of this process varies each year according to the development of the children. For instance, you can write dictated sentences at the beginning of the year. Later in the year, perhaps in January, ask the children to draw and write their news to bring to the whole group session. The children then read their news, while you write the news on the chart. In March, ask the children to write the predictable part

DAILY NEWS

of the news using interactive writing. Spelling approximations can be edited with the whole group using correction tape, labels, or adhesive notes. Closer to the end of the school year, allow the children to write their news on a large chart each day if they want to share. Again, allow the entire group to help edit the writing. Encourage the children to use many resources for finding correct spellings, such as word walls, word banks, dictionaries, class word lists, and so on.

Creating a News Book

Provide a news center in the classroom. Bind a news book for each child. Laminated local newspaper pages can serve as the front and back covers of the book. Pages from the book should be titled "My News" and "Headline News." News from the child, classroom, school, community, nation, or world can be used. Children draw or write their news on a daily basis. This news book serves as a record or journal of children's writing.

◆ PARENT CONNECTION

Send children home with a copy of the daily news, or e-mail an electronic version to parents and guardians who have e-mail. Using a hard copy of the daily news, ask children to "reread" the news to their parents and circle words they recognize. (Yes, this is preschool appropriate—it is the writing of the children's verbal sharing, which allows them to see that their words can be written.)

◆ ASSESSMENT

Use anecdotal records during daily news time to record children's approximations of writing and reading. For example, Austin says "hamburger" when shown a "McDonalds" label. This approximation signifies that Austin is making meaning from the label but is not yet using the phonetic cueing system.

◆ RELATED LITERATURE, SONGS, AND POEMS

Matthew Likes to Read, by J. Grainger
Reading Is Everywhere, by B. Cutting and J. Cutting

POSTERS AND SIGNS

 ◆ <u>**SUGGESTED GRADE LEVEL**</u>

PreK-2

 ◆ <u>**PURPOSE/RATIONALE**</u>

- ◆ Make connections between environmental print and the world
- ◆ Understand the functionality of print in the community setting, including signs, letters, newspapers, lists, messages, and menus
- ◆ Apply alphabetic knowledge to writing (Early Reading First goal)
- ◆ Develop print awareness (Early Reading First goal)

 ◆ <u>**MATERIALS**</u>

- ◆ Paper for posters
- ◆ Labels or copies of labels
- ◆ Markers, paint, and other writing tools

 ◆ <u>**PROCEDURE**</u>

Use environmental print to make labels related to the daily activities of the children.

Examples

- ◆ Mrs. Smith's Delivery Service: Children can learn about economics by providing a delivery service for the school. An older peer can be assigned to accompany a young child to make school deliveries that need to be made each day using an available wagon or cart. For example, any boxes delivered by mail or courier to the main office of the school can be placed in a wagon and delivered to the appropriate classrooms. The signs made for the delivery service help the school faculty and children to know about the service.
- ◆ Snack Area/Snack Bar: Ask children to make or purchase from local stores the signs needed for opening and closing the snack center in the classroom. Signs can be made or purchased that read "Yes, We Are Open" or "Sorry, We Are Closed." Through the use of related signs, children understand the functionality of print and its use in their daily lives.
- ◆ Wanted or Missing Posters: Children can use these posters when animals, books, or other classroom materials are missing. The children can hang the posters around the school so that others will know where to return missing items.
- ◆ Wanted Posters for Good Readers or Writers: Have the children attach a self-portrait or digital photograph of themselves to a poster and list their favorite book or piece of writing. This act helps the children see

POSTERS AND SIGNS

themselves as good readers and indicates what they are reading. Hang the posters in the classroom or hallway. Children can also use the posters to recommend favorite authors.

◆ Posters to Announce Upcoming Events: Engage the children in poster making for school-related events, such as a class play or grade-level event (a circus parade, book fair, soup label collection, etc.).

◆ VARIATIONS/EXTENSIONS

Make "I Can Read" posters. Have each child make a poster that includes the labels, logos, names, signs, and other materials that the child can read. Display the posters in the room so that the children can add to the list as the year progresses.

◆ PARENT CONNECTION

After children make their posters, they can display them in the classroom or take them home to share with their parents. Ask parents to discuss the experience the child had with the environmental print.

◆ ASSESSMENT

For each child, add the environmental print words used in the poster to the list of words the child recognizes. One example of organizing the words children recognize is *Words I Use When I Write*, by A. Trisler.

◆ RELATED LITERATURE, SONGS, AND POEMS

ABC Drive!, by N. Rowland

Freight Train, by D. Crews

I Read Signs, by T. Hoban

I Read Symbols, by T. Hoban

Light, by D. Crews

Matthew Likes to Read, by J. Grainger

The Signmaker's Assistant, by T. Arnold

Truck, by D. Crews

DICTIONARIES

◆ <u>**SUGGESTED GRADE LEVEL**</u>

PreK–2

◆ <u>**PURPOSE/RATIONALE**</u>

- ◆ Develop writing skills of English language learners and children with special needs by using dictionaries to learn about vocabulary and word sounds
- ◆ Develop phonological awareness to discriminate auditorily similar and different phonetic sounds (Early Reading First goal)
- ◆ Develop alphabetic knowledge by making connections between corresponding letters and sounds as they are used in environmental print
- ◆ Build phonological awareness through speaking and listening (Early Reading First goal)

◆ <u>**MATERIALS**</u>

- ◆ Paper stapled or bound in book form
- ◆ Environmental print brought in by the children
- ◆ Scissors and glue

◆ <u>**PROCEDURE**</u>

Label each page of the dictionary with a different letter of the alphabet, A through Z. Children then find environmental print labels and logos that have the same beginning sound as the corresponding alphabet letter and cut and paste the labels to the page. For example, children might glue a McDonald's logo on the M page. Place the dictionaries in a convenient place, such as a workstation or center for easy access.

◆ <u>**VARIATIONS/EXTENSIONS**</u>

- ◆ Make a class alphabet book, in addition to individual dictionaries.
- ◆ Develop word boxes with the children. Children glue or copy environmental print words or other words needed for writing onto index cards. Children then place the cards in a plastic index card box divided with alphabet tabs. Additions to this resource should be ongoing during the school year.

◆ <u>**PARENT CONNECTION**</u>

This activity can be completed at home for homework or as a suggested activity for parents and children.

DICTIONARIES

◆ ASSESSMENT

By reviewing individual dictionaries, you can record the number of letters a child has filled in successfully.

Name of Child Austin	Aa Arby's	Bb Burger King	Cc Coca-Cola
Dd Dunkin Donuts	Ee Eggo	Ff	Gg
Hh	Ii	Jj	Kk
Ll	Mm	Nn	Oo
Pp	Qq	Rr	Ss
Tt	Uu	Vv	Ww
Xx	Yy	Zz	

◆ RELATED LITERATURE, SONGS, AND POEMS

ABC Drive!, by N. Howland

WRITING EXPERIENCES

◆ SUGGESTED GRADE LEVEL

PreK–2

◆ PURPOSE/RATIONALE

- ◆ Gain experience in reading and writing environmental print in manuscript or a different context depending on each child's level of literacy development
- ◆ Demonstrate alphabetic knowledge by writing about self-selected items and accompanying experiences (Early Reading First goal)

◆ MATERIALS

- ◆ Environmental print
- ◆ Various kinds of paper
- ◆ Pencils, pens, markers, crayons, and other writing tools

◆ PROCEDURE

Children select labels or logos that they can read or that they know about and glue them on a sheet of paper. Children then write about their selections. A preschooler might draw a picture and write only a couple of letters. A second grader might write several sentences about his or her experiences with a logo. Share the writing as a group or display it in the room.

◆ PARENT CONNECTION

Allow children to make individual books with writing examples to share with their parents.

◆ ASSESSMENT

Use a writing rubric to assess each child's level of writing development:

Level 1—Emerging: mostly scribbling

Level 2—Pictorial: draws pictures that could be recognizable; can tell a story from the picture; may insert some writing symbols

Level 3—Precommunicative: includes letter strings or preletter symbols; occasionally inserts name or known words; tells a story from the writing

Level 4—Semiphonetic: shows some letter-sound association; writes one letter for each word; writes from left to right with occasional reversals

Level 5—Phonetic: includes beginning and ending sounds; uses some high-frequency words; can write one or two sentences

WRITING EXPERIENCES

Level 6—Transitional: spells high-frequency words correctly; writes medial sounds of words, including some vowels; uses some punctuation; writes multiple sentences

Level 7—Conventional: spells high-frequency words correctly; uses some correctly spelled vocabulary and some phonetic spelling; varies sentence structure; uses correct punctuation; includes spaces between words

SOURCE: Adapted from Feldgus and Cardonick (1999).

Child's Name	Level 1 Emerging	Level 2 Pictorial	Level 3 Precommunicative	Level 4 Semiphonetic	Level 5 Phonetic	Level 6 Transitional	Level 7 Conventional
Austin			September		February		

VARIATIONS/EXTENSIONS

◆ This is a good contribution to the child's portfolio. Allow the children to select pieces of writing that they think show their progress throughout the year.
◆ Use multiple forms of writing in the classroom, including shared or interactive writing, with you as well as with other children; guided writing, in which you help individual children or small groups to edit and revise their writing; and independent writing, with children using opportunities to explore and experiment with writing on topics of their choice.

RELATED LITERATURE, SONGS, AND POEMS

Matthew Likes to Read, by J. Grainger
Reading Is Everywhere, by B. Cutting and J. Cutting

LITERACY ACROSS THEMATIC UNITS

◆ SUGGESTED GRADE LEVEL

PreK-2

◆ PURPOSE/RATIONALE

- ◆ Make connections between school and the world
- ◆ Demonstrate the ability to use environmental print in multiple meaningful contexts

◆ MATERIALS

- ◆ Materials related to chosen thematic units
- ◆ Environmental print labels and logos

◆ PROCEDURE

Select thematic units that incorporate state and local requirements and children's interests. Depending on the topic, determine how environmental print can contribute to the children's understandings of literacy related to the topic. Stories, songs, bulletin boards, class-made books, murals, graphs, lists, recipes, and so on can incorporate environmental print labels and logos. Through the following examples, children can develop fine motor skills, refine classification and word recognition skills, and develop vocabulary.

Insect Unit

Fill a large paper picnic basket with things children might like to eat at a picnic. Research why insects are attracted to some foods more than others. This knowledge builds children's prior knowledge and experience with research on particular topics.

"Me" Unit

Children draw a silhouette of themselves on butcher paper and cut it out. They then glue their favorite foods and drinks on the silhouette to display in the classroom. This activity builds fine motor skills and print awareness.

Celebrations Unit

Using the cultures represented in the classroom, incorporate environmental print related to diverse cultural celebrations.

Weather Unit

Compare and contrast hot and cold weather through food, clothing, drinks, and machines. Through this activity, children learn about contrasts in temperature in the local community. Class graphs noting daily temperatures can expose children to varied ways to represent data.

LITERACY ACROSS THEMATIC UNITS

Farm Unit

Find foods that come from different places on a farm. For example, a McDonald's hamburger comes from a cow, whereas McDonald's French fries come from a plant. Seed packages can be used as additional environmental print reading. Through this activity, children build oral language related to a farm. Children can then use this language to write about a farm.

Ocean Unit

Find foods that come from the ocean. Make menus for restaurants. Through this activity, children develop content language related to the ocean.

Transportation Unit

Read *Trucks,* by Donald Crews, to the class. Children trace and cut patterns of trucks and then select labels or logos to go on the sides of the trucks. Through this activity, children develop fine motor skills and print awareness.

◆ VARIATIONS/EXTENSIONS

Include environmental print in math activities related to the thematic unit. For example, have children estimate or count the number of objects in an estimation jar.

◆ PARENT CONNECTION

Keep parents informed through a newsletter about particular topics of study—topics either scheduled in lesson plans or spontaneously emerging. Encourage parents to discuss with their child aspects of the classroom theme, sending related environmental print to the class when appropriate.

◆ ASSESSMENT

Depending on the curricular area, record pertinent information about children's use of language related to the activity. Artifacts made by the children can be included in individual portfolios.

◆ RELATED LITERATURE, SONGS, AND POEMS

Any books, songs, and poems gathered for thematic units can be used.

REBUS STORIES

 SUGGESTED GRADE LEVEL

PreK–2

 PURPOSE/RATIONALE

- ◆ Learn about writing through language experience events in the classroom
- ◆ Demonstrate the ability to categorize appropriate environmental print to use in rebus stories

 MATERIALS

- ◆ Familiar literature
- ◆ Appropriate environmental print labels and logos

 PROCEDURE

Select a story that is familiar to the children. Write a parallel story inserting environmental print when appropriate. Have the children illustrate the story to display. For example, children might write that Cinderella had to clean the floors with Spic and Span and that Cinderella's stepsisters were fat and ugly because they ate too many Chips Ahoy cookies and Lay's potato chips. Cinderella went to the ball at Hardee's in a Toyota. Little Caesar's danced with Cinderella all night. Cinderella left her Converse shoe at the ball. Cinderella and the prince served Danish Wedding Cookies and Kool-Aid at their wedding.

 VARIATIONS/EXTENSIONS

Try a book used for shared reading to incorporate environmental print (rhyme, rhythm, repetition), such as a book from the *Meanies* collection, by J. Cowley.

 PARENT CONNECTION

Parents will enjoy reading class books that are sent home. Consider allowing each child to select a class book to take home as an artifact at the end of the school year.

 ASSESSMENT

Make anecdotal records about the children's abilities to retell stories.

 RELATED LITERATURE, SONGS, AND POEMS

"I Like Bugs," by M. W. Brown
"Today Is Monday," by E. Carle
The Very Hungry Caterpillar, by E. Carle

WALL LISTS AND BULLETIN BOARDS

 SUGGESTED GRADE LEVEL

PreK–2

 PURPOSE/RATIONALE

- ◆ Understand the functionality of print in our world
- ◆ Develop print awareness

 MATERIALS

- ◆ Bulletin board paper
- ◆ Environmental print labels and logos

PROCEDURE

Use a bulletin board or a large piece of bulletin board paper to keep ongoing lists of environmental print. List titles might include the following:

- ◆ Places We Like to Eat
- ◆ Things We Like to Eat
- ◆ Places We Like to Go
- ◆ Words We Can Read
- ◆ Signs We Can Read
- ◆ Our Favorite Snacks
- ◆ Places in Our Community

Let children make individual lists (e.g., "Places I Like to Eat") and post them in an easily accessible area so the children can update the lists regularly. Hallways outside the classroom are a great place for displaying these lists. Class graphs that incorporate environmental print can also be used.

 PARENT CONNECTION

Encourage parents to make similar lists at home, possibly displaying them on the refrigerator or in their child's room. Notify parents of lists generated at school, so they can contribute relevant environmental print from home.

 ASSESSMENT

Observe children's attempts to read as they "read around the room." When children read around the room they use pointers to practice reading familiar text displayed in the classroom. Another option for reading around the room is to provide clipboards, pencils, and paper for children to use as they look for words related to phonics skills being taught in the class. For instance, children might look for words that begin with the letter *C*. Children write the words they find on a sheet of paper, which can then be used for assessment.

◆ RELATED LITERATURE, SONGS, AND POEMS

Matthew Likes to Read, by J. Grainger

POCKET CHARTS

 ◆ <u>**SUGGESTED GRADE LEVEL**</u>

PreK–2

 ◆ <u>**PURPOSE/RATIONALE**</u>

- ◆ Participate in repeated experiences with familiar print
- ◆ Develop phonological awareness by rhyming, blending, and segmenting sounds, syllables, and words (Early Reading First goal)

 ◆ <u>**MATERIALS**</u>

- ◆ Pocket chart
- ◆ Environmental print logos and labels
- ◆ Sentence strips

◆ <u>**PROCEDURE**</u>

Use the pocket chart to display labels the children bring to class. This pocket chart can be used in a developmental progression of print awareness, depending on the age of the child and his or her level of print exposure (pocket charts are most effective when used in a developmental progression; McCracken & McCracken, 1986).

Day 1/Level 1—Match the original label to another original label of the same product

Day 2/Level 2—Match the original label to a black and white copy of the original label

Day 3/Level 3—Match the original label to the original label with all context removed

Day 4/Level 4—Match the original label with the manuscript of the label's words

Day 5/Level 5—Use print from the label in a sentence written on a sentence strip and used in a pocket chart; have children highlight the environmental print word

 ◆ <u>**VARIATIONS/EXTENSIONS**</u>

Display sentences children have dictated about the environmental print in the pocket chart. After some exposure to the sentences, cut the sentences into phrases and let the children practice putting the parts back together. After exposure to the phrases, sentence strips can be cut into words for children to reconstruct.

POCKET CHARTS

PARENT CONNECTION

Allow children to take the sentence strips home in plastic bags to practice constructing and deconstructing text.

ASSESSMENT

Observe children as they interact with the pocket chart during independent exploration. If used as a whole-group time activity, record children's success in constructing and deconstructing text. Determine the level of print awareness of each child through the following checklist. Notice that each child's knowledge of individual labels is recorded by date. Criteria for levels can be found in the Procedure section of this activity.

Name: Susie Jones

Environmental Print	Level 1	Level 2	Level 3	Level 4	Level 5
McDonald's	9-1	9-20	10-15	1-17	1-30
Coca-Cola	9-1				
Stop	9-1				
Doritos					

RELATED LITERATURE, SONGS, AND POEMS

See Resource A and the References section.

TEXT INNOVATIONS

◆ SUGGESTED GRADE LEVEL

PreK–3

◆ PURPOSE/RATIONALE

- ◆ Build print awareness through repeated readings of a class book
- ◆ Reread familiar texts
- ◆ Learn concepts about print and build fluency by rereading familiar texts
- ◆ Develop phonological awareness, including rhyming, blending, and segmenting sounds through interaction with text (Early Reading First goal)
- ◆ Increase oral language skills by discussing story innovations created with environmental print (Early Reading First goal)
- ◆ Retell familiar stories and increase comprehension skills

◆ MATERIALS

- ◆ Poster paper
- ◆ Tagboard
- ◆ Environmental print labels, logos, and signs
- ◆ 12" × 18" construction paper
- ◆ Glue
- ◆ Markers, crayons, and paint

◆ PROCEDURE

Select a text that is familiar to the children, such as a song, chant, poem, or book, using environmental print labels when appropriate. For example, children might use environmental print to complete a familiar text, similar to a cloze procedure:

> Little witch, little witch,
> What do you eat?
> I eat _____ for a treat.

Let the children illustrate the book and bind it for a class book or display it for children to read and write around the room.

The children can add any illustrations needed. Wall displays can later be taken down and made into a class book. Read and reread the book with the class to expose children to words in their original contexts and in manuscript or type.

◆ VARIATIONS/EXTENSIONS

Have students invent their own extensions of books, for instance:

> Billy, Billy, what do you eat?
> I eat at *McDonalds* for a treat.

TEXT INNOVATIONS

Through this activity, children can retell familiar stories and build comprehension as stories are revisited.

Individual books can be made for children to use in small groups or for independent reading. Struggling readers especially enjoy texts made with familiar print.

Use the book *A, My Name Is Alice,* by Jane Bayer. Make sentence strips or a book using the child's name and a label that begins with the same beginning sound—for example, "T, my name is Tiara, and I sell Teddy Grahams" (using the label from the Teddy Grahams box).

◆ PARENT CONNECTION

Allow children to take class books home for repeated readings with parents to practice fluency.

◆ ASSESSMENT

Note children's engagement with print, including sight words and fluency, as you examine pages of the class book. Consider using Marie Clay's (2002) *An Observation Survey of Early Literacy Achievement* to identify concepts about print. Make a class grid like the one that follows to show which concepts can be taught.

	Front of book	Begins on left of page	Return sweep	Holds book and turns pages	Distinguishes print from picture	Punctuation	Letter recognition	One-to-one correspondence
Timmy	x	x	x	x	x	x	x	x
David	x			x	x		x	
Alisha		x		x				
Tiara	x	x		x	x	x	x	x
Satomi	x			x	x			

◆ RELATED LITERATURE, SONGS, AND POEMS

A, My Name Is Alice, by J. Bayer
"Have You Ever Been to Kmart?" in *Eating the Alphabet,* by L. Ehlert
Lazy Mary, by J. Melser
Meanies collection, by J. Cowley
On Market Street, by A. Lobel

WORD BOXES

WORD BOXES

◆ SUGGESTED GRADE LEVEL

PreK–2

◆ PURPOSE/RATIONALE

- ◆ Organize and use words needed for reading and writing
- ◆ Develop oral language by recording new words to use when speaking and writing (Early Reading First goal)
- ◆ Develop alphabetic knowledge by recording and alphabetizing words in word boxes (Early Reading First goal)

◆ MATERIALS

- ◆ Index card box
- ◆ Index cards
- ◆ Tabbed alphabet cards for index box
- ◆ Environmental print labels
- ◆ Glue

◆ PROCEDURE

As children accumulate a sight word vocabulary, write the words on index cards to keep in a word box. These words can include environmental print also. For each new word learned, glue the environmental print label and the word written in manuscript on the index card and file the card under the word's beginning letter.

◆ VARIATIONS/EXTENSIONS

During writing time in the classroom, encourage children to use their word boxes when they need to know how to spell a word. Use a word wall or word bank to list words the class wants to know how to spell. These words might be high-frequency words, thematic words, or environmental print. If you use a word wall, place library card pockets under each category of words, with the words written on sentence strips for easy access.

Names	Weather	Pet Words	Environmental Print
Susie	sunny	dog	McDonalds
Billy	cloudy	cat	Coca-Cola
Jaceka	windy	rabbit	Burger King
Antoine	cold	gerbil	Doritos
Sitomi	hot	fish	stop

WORD BOXES

WORD BOXES

 ◆ **PARENT CONNECTION**

Allow the children to occasionally take their word boxes home. Share the word boxes at parent conferences and ask parents to contribute words they notice their children using when reading and writing.

 ◆ **ASSESSMENT**

Check the word boxes when conferencing with children.

◆ **RELATED LITERATURE, SONGS, AND POEMS**

The Alphabet Tree, by L. Lionni

BOOK BOXES

BOOK BOXES

SUGGESTED GRADE LEVEL

PreK–2

PURPOSE/RATIONALE

- ◆ Build fluency through repeated readings of familiar text found in a book box (Reading First goal)
- ◆ Use environmental print as part of classroom routines
- ◆ Enhance oral language by rereading familiar texts (Early Reading First goal)

MATERIALS

- ◆ Sturdy boxes displaying logos, such as detergent and cereal boxes

PROCEDURE

Store a child's favorite books, books to be practiced, and books written by the child in sturdy boxes. Books found in the book boxes can be fiction or nonfiction, depending on the child's interests and exposure to varying genres. The books can be at the child's frustration, instructional, or independent level:

- ◆ Frustration level—Children read less than 90% of the text independently. However, some books have a strong story line with supporting illustrations. Children can use these illustrations to make up stories or retell stories the teacher might have read during a read-aloud experience.
- ◆ Instructional level—Children read 90% to 94% of the text accurately. These books contain enough supports and challenges within the text to support readers' problem-solving attempts.
- ◆ Independent level—Children read 95% to 100% of the text accurately. These texts are easy for children to decode and comprehend.

VARIATIONS/EXTENSIONS

Boxes can also be used to store collections of books by a particular author, books of a particular genre, or books used for thematic study.

PARENT CONNECTION

Books or stories read by children should be sent home to be read to parents or guardians. A record of the books, with spaces for comments from the parents, is a nice way to include parental input.

BOOK BOXES

ASSESSMENT

Keep reading records of the books children choose for independent reading. Knowledge of each child's instructional reading level will help you provide reading materials at an appropriate level.

Reading Record

Child's Name	Date	Book Name	Skill Practiced	Parent Signature

RELATED LITERATURE, SONGS, AND POEMS

See Resource A and the References section.

NEWSPAPER AD WORD SEARCH

◆ SUGGESTED GRADE LEVEL

PreK–2

◆ PURPOSE/RATIONALE

- ◆ Increase the number of words read through repeated exposure to environmental print in varied contexts
- ◆ Use alphabetic knowledge of letters and sounds to problem solve with words (Early Reading First goal)
- ◆ Develop print awareness through the use of newspaper ads (Early Reading First goal)

◆ MATERIALS

- ◆ Weekly store ads from the newspaper, such as ads from local grocery stores, department stores, and catalogs

◆ PROCEDURE

During group time, have children circle words they can read in newspaper ads. Many of the ads have accompanying pictures to give children clues, and some of the ads are in color.

◆ VARIATIONS/EXTENSIONS

Keep an ad displayed in the children's reach or in a literacy center, so they can independently look for words they can read during the day. Place ads in a newspaper or environmental print center to give children the opportunity to use functional print. For example, children can use ads to make grocery lists or lists of items needed for classroom snacks and cooking experiences.

◆ PARENT CONNECTION

Remind parents to call their child's attention to ads in the local newspaper as they go about their daily routines.

◆ ASSESSMENT

Provide children with blank books bound with laminated pages of the newspaper. These books can be placed in the newspaper center or the environmental print center. Children can cut and paste familiar words from newspapers into the blank book to provide a record of progress in word recognition. Check these books periodically to record the children's progress.

 ## RELATED LITERATURE, SONGS, AND POEMS

Matthew Likes to Read, by J. Grainger

NEWSPAPER AD WORD SEARCH

NEWSPAPER AD WORD SEARCH

RECIPES

◆ **SUGGESTED GRADE LEVEL**

PreK–3

◆ **PURPOSE/RATIONALE**

- ◆ Learn that print has a function.
- ◆ Become familiar with measurement (mathematics) and changing states of matter (physics) through cooking
- ◆ Learn new vocabulary related to cooking (Reading First goal)
- ◆ Learn to follow a sequence of activities

◆ **MATERIALS**

- ◆ Chart tablet or index cards
- ◆ Recipes for snacks and other cooking activities
- ◆ Labels from ingredients used in snacks and recipes

◆ **PROCEDURE**

Write a simple recipe on a chart tablet or index cards. Use labels to illustrate ingredients whenever possible. Read the recipe with the children.

◆ **VARIATIONS/EXTENSIONS**

Children may want to think of their own recipes for surprise dishes. It is always good to duplicate or make copies of the recipes that are used in the classroom for the children to practice reading.

Initiate a classroom recipe book that contains the recipes cooked in the classroom throughout the year. Use the recipe book as a gift for parents or as a way to earn money for classroom books.

Write the recipe steps on sentence strips and ask the children to place them in correct sequential order.

◆ **PARENT CONNECTION**

Any recipes used in the classroom can be typed and sent home for parents to try.

◆ **ASSESSMENT**

Allow each child to compile recipes used in the classroom for an individual recipe book. Periodically check the recipe books to be sure that each child has compiled the class recipes over the year. Depending on the

RECIPES

developmental level of the child, provide a structured recipe format that children can use to fill in with familiar print.

Peanut Butter and Jelly Sandwiches

2 pieces of _____ (bread)

1 spoonful of _____ (peanut butter)

1 spoonful of _____ (jelly)

Spread peanut butter and jelly on bread. Put the two pieces of bread together. Use the cookie cutters in the snack center to cut your sandwich into your favorite shape. Eat and enjoy!

Check each child's spelling progress throughout the year.

◆ RELATED LITERATURE, SONGS, AND POEMS

"The Easter Kitchen" (poem), by B. Bagert
Cook-a-doodle-doo, by J. Stevens

LUNCHBOXES

LUNCHBOXES

◆ SUGGESTED GRADE LEVEL

PreK–2

◆ PURPOSE/RATIONALE

- ◆ Become familiar with the Food Pyramid and concepts of nutrition
- ◆ Categorize foods using the Food Pyramid
- ◆ Read and identify the label or logo to correctly place it on the Pyramid or lunchbox
- ◆ Develop oral language by discussing and learning about different foods (Early Reading First goal)

◆ MATERIALS

- ◆ Tagboard or poster board for lunchboxes
- ◆ Bulletin board paper for Food Pyramid mural
- ◆ Scissors and glue
- ◆ Environmental print labels from food boxes and cans
- ◆ Construction paper

◆ PROCEDURE

Have the children decorate lunchboxes cut from the tagboard or poster board. Then have them select food labels of the foods they like to see in their lunchboxes. Children should use their knowledge of the Food Pyramid to be sure that their lunchbox represents a balanced meal.

If the students use a mural for the Food Pyramid, hang a large triangle-shaped paper on the wall. Divide the triangle into food groups. Glue the labels children bring to class in their appropriate food group category. Write the name of the label or logo in manuscript, or place a typed version, under each label so that children are exposed to the print in varied contexts.

◆ VARIATIONS/EXTENSIONS

Make lunchboxes that have nutritious foods and lunchboxes that have junk food. Discuss good choices in the Food Pyramid, such as fruits, vegetables, protein, and grains. Title a display "You Are What You Eat" for children to post their lunchbox choices.

◆ PARENT CONNECTION

Encourage parents to allow children to accompany them on a trip to the grocery store and point out labels and logos.

<u>ASSESSMENT</u>

As children categorize items on the Food Pyramid or on the lunchbox, assess their knowledge of word identification and classification by noting children's selections, categorization skills, and ability to read the labels and logos. Compile an ongoing list of words the children are consistently using in reading and writing.

 <u>RELATED LITERATURE, SONGS, AND POEMS</u>

"How to Say No Politely When a Lion Invites You to Lunch" (poem), by B. Bagert

BILLBOARDS

◆ SUGGESTED GRADE LEVEL

PreK–2

◆ PURPOSE/RATIONALE

- ◆ Recognize print in many contexts
- ◆ Use descriptive oral language and writing when inventing slogans or other marketing devices to use with environmental print (Early Reading First goal)

◆ MATERIALS

- ◆ One fourth of a sheet of poster paper per child
- ◆ Environmental print labels
- ◆ Toilet tissue rolls or paper towel rolls

◆ PROCEDURE

Have the children select a label to use when making a billboard. Slogans used by the manufacturer of the product or those composed by the children are written and placed with the label on the billboard. For preK children, write child-dictated slogans for billboards. Attach the toilet or paper towel rolls to the billboard by making two 1-inch slits on one end of the roll and inserting the poster board into the slits. Secure the rolls with a small amount of glue if needed. The poster board serves as the billboard; the rolls serve as the pole supports that hold up the billboard.

◆ VARIATIONS/EXTENSIONS

Shoe box tops can also be used effectively. Attach them to tissue rolls by stapling.

Make a billboard alphabet. Collaborate with the children to think of an entire set of billboards that correspond with the letters of the alphabet—for example, for Pizza Hut the billboard could read "Makin' It Great."

◆ PARENT CONNECTION

Encourage parents to play alphabet games or "I Spy" when traveling with children by finding letters of the alphabet on billboards and signs.

◆ ASSESSMENT

The finished billboard can be used as evidence of children's attempts with writing. Note the billboards that each child constructs to gain information related to individual letters and sounds used in the contexts of familiar labels and logos. Billboards should be remade each year to ensure they reflect the local community.

 ◆ **RELATED LITERATURE, SONGS, AND POEMS**

Light, by D. Crews
The Signmaker's Assistant, by T. Arnold

ALPHABET SCAVENGER HUNT

◆ SUGGESTED GRADE LEVEL

PreK–2

◆ PURPOSE/RATIONALE

◆ Actively locate alphabet letters around the classroom
◆ Develop alphabetic knowledge (Early Reading First goal)

◆ MATERIALS

◆ Memos copied for each child (e.g., "Find a label, sign, or logo that begins with the letter D. Bring it to school.")

◆ PROCEDURE

Using the available environmental print in the classroom, ask the children to find labels and logos that begin with selected letters of the alphabet. Additionally, look for other words in the classroom that begin with that letter. Record the information on letter sheets to be compiled into individual alphabet books.

◆ VARIATIONS/EXTENSIONS

Label 26 shoe boxes or plastic boxes with one letter of the alphabet. Ask the children to find small objects, pictures, environmental print labels and logos, or nonperishable food items to place in the boxes according to the beginning sound of the letter on the box. For instance, an S box might contain salt, scissors, soup, seashells, a ship, the number six, Skittles, and so on. As an ancillary activity, write the names of the items on a sentence strip. These strips can also be used in a matching game. Another activity involves making a list titled "Can You Find . . . ?" which is placed on top of each box and lists the items in the box. Children can then search the boxes for each item.

Children can bring the labels from the boxes and containers of their favorite foods. Compare how many different beginning sounds are represented. Children can make up riddles for the labels they bring and let the other children guess the product name. One of the clues should always be the beginning letter or sound.

◆ PARENT CONNECTION

Children can take home a letter asking parents to help them fill their letter box with items from their home. Parents are welcome to send items as often as they like. If parents are unable to help their child, the children can use items from the classroom to fill their boxes. This activity is especially effective if the children do not seem interested in bringing in environmental print on a regular basis.

◆ ASSESSMENT

If children complete this activity independently or in small groups, their finished word list can provide information related to letter identification. Individual alphabet books provide evidence of individual progress in letter identification.

Scavenger Hunt Word Lists

Aa	Bb

◆ RELATED LITERATURE, SONGS, AND POEMS

It Begins With an A, by S. Calmenson
Messages in the Mailbox, by L. Leedy

ENVIRONMENTAL PRINT WALK

SUGGESTED GRADE LEVEL

PreK–2

PURPOSE/RATIONALE

♦ Develop print awareness and alphabetic knowledge (Early Reading First goal)

MATERIALS

♦ Clipboards
♦ Paper and pencils
♦ Cameras

PROCEDURE

A walk in and around the school is good any time of the year but especially at the beginning of the school year. Carrying clipboards, pencils, and paper, have children walk in and around the school searching for important signs and posters. Have the children copy the signs they encounter. Some children will draw pictures of the signs. Students can take pictures of the signs also. After returning to the classroom, work with the children to compile a class list and discuss what each sign says and its importance.

VARIATIONS/EXTENSIONS

After discussing all of the signs brought back by the children, determine signs that might be needed in the classroom—for example, "Stop," "Sorry, We're Closed," and "Exit." Encourage the children to make these signs.

Use the book *I Went Walking,* by Sue Williams, to make a class book about the environmental print walk. The text might read, "Joshua went walking. What did I see? I saw an exit sign looking at me."

Make an alphabet of the local community. Begin by asking the students to tell you the names of places they eat, shop, purchase gas, or worship. On a large chart, place each contribution beside the beginning letter of the alphabet.

Aa Arby's	**Dd** Days Inn
Bb Burger King	**Ee** Eckerds
Cc Citibank	**Ff** Food World

ENVIRONMENTAL PRINT WALK

Photographs can then be taken of each place. Beneath each letter, write the name of the business with a corresponding first letter and, below that, a photograph of the business.

◆ PARENT CONNECTION

Encourage parents to call attention to signs and symbols they see as they go to and from school each day. Compile a class list of signs in the community, based on family encounters with print. Make a class graph from the gathered information to see which signs appear the most and least in the community.

◆ ASSESSMENT

Examine the children's lists to see their ability to copy and possibly reread. Based on the class compilation of environmental print information, plan appropriate environmental print experiences.

◆ RELATED LITERATURE, SONGS, AND POEMS

ABC Drive!, by N. Howland
I Read Signs, by T. Hoban
I Read Symbols, by T. Hoban
I Went Walking, by S. Williams
Matthew Likes to Read, by J. Grainger
Reading Is Everywhere, by B. Cutting and J. Cutting
The Signmaker's Assistant, by T. Arnold
Signs, by B. Cutting and J. Cutting
The Tale of Thomas Mead, by P. Hutchins

RESTAURANT MENUS

 ## SUGGESTED GRADE LEVEL

PreK–2

 ## PURPOSE/RATIONALE

- ◆ Understand that print is used for many different purposes
- ◆ Understand the diversity of culture found in the United States
- ◆ Develop print awareness (Early Reading First goal)
- ◆ Develop fine motor skills

 ## MATERIALS

- ◆ Menus from various types of restaurants
- ◆ Paper, glue, scissors
- ◆ Magazines with pictures of food

 ## PROCEDURE

Provide children with various menus from local restaurants. Allow children to cut pictures of foods from the magazines to make their own menus. They can write the names of the entrées as well as the prices. Include menus from restaurants that feature foods from many cultures, such as Chinese, Thai, Japanese, Indian, Italian, Mexican, and Filipino restaurants. If the menus include more than one language, obtain a copy in both languages, if possible. Children can examine the differences in print between the different languages.

 ## VARIATIONS/EXTENSIONS

The children might like to set up the classroom or part of the classroom as a restaurant. Menus can be posted in these areas. Children can use pads, pencils, aprons, and cash registers as props. Children can also make self-portraits, attaching a copy of a menu from their favorite restaurant.

Check the school cafeteria menu each day. Have children cut pictures from magazines to represent the items served in the cafeteria for that day. Have children paste the pictures on index cards and print or type the names of the items beneath the pictures. For organization and reuse of this activity, punch holes in the cards and place the cards on a ring. Hang the ring beside the menu for the day so that children can see the foods for the day and the associated language associated. All children enjoy participating in and using this useful activity in the classroom.

Make a class graph of favorite restaurants.

RESTAURANT MENUS

◆ PARENT CONNECTION

Ask parents to point out familiar print on menus when they eat at restaurants with their children. If possible, ask the children to bring in a sample menu. Also, when cooking at home, have parents ask children to write the items to be included in the meal, using any available labels or logos.

◆ ASSESSMENT

Menus made by children are evidence of their knowledge of familiar labels and logos. Include menus as part of a child's portfolio to show children's use of varied contexts when reading and writing.

◆ RELATED LITERATURE, SONGS, AND POEMS

"Fancy Restaurants" (poem), by B. Bagert
Pigs Will Be Pigs, by A. Axelrod

ALPHABET WALL/COMMUNITY ALPHABET

SUGGESTED GRADE LEVEL

PreK–3

PURPOSE/RATIONALE

- ◆ Develop phonological awareness by auditorily and visually associating beginning letters and sounds with locations in the community (Reading First goal)
- ◆ Develop alphabetic knowledge (Early Reading First goal)
- ◆ Develop oral language related to the community (Early Reading First goal)

MATERIALS

- ◆ Blank alphabet cards (one fourth or one half of a sheet of poster board)
- ◆ Environmental print brought in by the children
- ◆ Environmental print alphabet book (teacher made or made by a previous class)
- ◆ Cameras

PROCEDURE

Start the school year with alphabet cards that display only letters. As the children bring in environmental print, match the print to the letters. Tape or glue the labels and logos to the cards that begin with matching letters. For example, the card with the letter G could be matched with the logo for Green Giant. Use a teacher-made alphabet book or a book made by a previous class as a model to show children what is meant by environmental print.

Photographs of landmarks in the community, such as parks, statues, shopping malls, department stores, grocery stores, toy stores, and so on, can be taken with a digital camera. Photos can then be printed onto large cards and used to make a community alphabet. Be sure that all photographs used are common to your locality. This alphabet may change from time to time as communities change.

VARIATIONS/EXTENSIONS

Take the photographs for the community alphabet during the summer. Let the children choose the photographs that they would like to use for the alphabet.

Use photographs of people, signs, and places in the school to make a school alphabet.

◆ **PARENT CONNECTION**

Encourage parents to allow their children to write the names of establishments in the community frequented by their family. Children can make their own environmental print alphabet book at home.

◆ **ASSESSMENT**

As children compile possible items to go on the alphabet cards, note their knowledge of beginning sounds using a checklist, such as the following list.

Harrison's Alphabet

Aa	Bb Burger King	Cc California Pizza Kitchen	Dd	Ee Enrique's Mexican Cuisine
Fe Ferraro's				

◆ **RELATED LITERATURE, SONGS, AND POEMS**

ABC Drive!, by N. Rowland

ALPHABET BOOKS

◆ SUGGESTED GRADE LEVEL

PreK–2

◆ PURPOSE/RATIONALE

- ◆ Have fun opportunities to learn the letters of the alphabet
- ◆ Actively engage in developing alphabetic knowledge (Early Reading First goal)

◆ MATERIALS

- ◆ Various alphabet books
- ◆ Glue, scissors, markers
- ◆ Environmental print brought in by the children
- ◆ Paper to make books

◆ PROCEDURE

Using the format of a favorite alphabet book, make a class alphabet book. For example, *Eating the Alphabet,* by Lois Ehlert, provides a good format for the children to make their own alphabet book using labels, logos, and signs (you can also use *A, My Name Is Alice,* by Jane Bayer as a format for a class book). Display the names of the labels in manuscript or type.

◆ VARIATIONS/EXTENSIONS

Make individual alphabet books.

◆ PARENT CONNECTION

Encourage parents to spend time making an alphabet book at home using environmental print. Children can then bring the books to school and read them to the class.

Place child-made alphabet books in the classroom library or ask the media specialist in your school to display books made by the children.

◆ ASSESSMENT

Individual alphabet books are evidence of beginning letter and sound knowledge and phonemic awareness.

◆ RELATED LITERATURE, SONGS, AND POEMS

ABC Drive!, by N. Howland
Eating the Alphabet, by L. Ehlert

READING INSIDE THE BOX

READING INSIDE THE BOX

◆ SUGGESTED GRADE LEVEL

PreK-2

◆ PURPOSE/RATIONALE

- ◆ Read independently and privately
- ◆ Develop print awareness and reading fluency (Early Reading First and Reading First goals)
- ◆ Practice mathematical skills such as estimation

◆ MATERIALS

- ◆ Refrigerator box or any large box
- ◆ Cereal boxes
- ◆ Scissors
- ◆ Glue

◆ PROCEDURE

Cover the outside of a large box with cereal box fronts. Provide children opportunities to read in the box. Place a bin or basket of books inside the box to encourage children's participation. This large box can be used inside the classroom or outside the classroom door.

◆ VARIATIONS/EXTENSIONS

Before covering the box, ask the children to estimate how many cereal box fronts would be needed to cover the box. During the covering of the box, periodically ask the children to count the number of box fronts used. Ask the children to adjust their estimates. After covering the box, give the children a sheet with a list of cereal types used on the reading box. Ask children to count the total used. Which type of cereal was used the most? The least? The reading box can be placed in an environmental print area of the class, in a classroom library, or just outside the door of the classroom.

◆ PARENT CONNECTION

Send a letter home to parents explaining the activity, so they will save cereal boxes and send them to the classroom.

◆ ASSESSMENT

Evidence of problem solving seen in the children's work can be included in a math journal or portfolio.

Name:
Which cereal brand appears the most on the reading box?
Total number of most brands used:
Which cereal brand appears the least on the reading box?
Total number of least brands used:
Which cereal brand is your favorite?
How many boxes of your favorite brand are on the reading box?
How many cereal boxes are needed to cover one side of the reading box?
How many cereal boxes are on the reading box in all?

 RELATED LITERATURE, SONGS, AND POEMS

See Resource A and the References section.

Math Activities

Environmental print is not just for language arts. There are numerous activities to be used in conjunction with math. Some children, even some preschoolers, are afraid of mathematics. However, math can be less scary when environmental print is used with both typically developing children and children with special needs. Environmental print instruction has been investigated with children who received special education services. Aldridge and Rust (1987) found that first-grade children with mental retardation enrolled in special education classes benefited from environmental print instruction. The children saw themselves as active learners and were proactive in seeking out print in the environment.

The following pages offer a number of activities that children can enjoy while developing both mathematics and literacy skills:

There are numerous environmental print activities to be used in conjunction with math.

PUZZLES

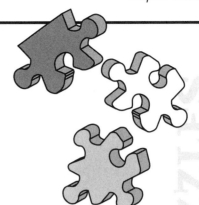

◆ SUGGESTED GRADE LEVEL

PreK–1

◆ PURPOSE/RATIONALE

- ◆ Develop spatial knowledge
- ◆ Attend to the conventions of print

◆ MATERIALS

- ◆ Boxes from detergents, cereals, department stores, and so forth
- ◆ Plastic sandwich bags

◆ PROCEDURE

Cut boxes into four to six pieces to make a puzzle. Put the pieces in a plastic sandwich bag. Store the puzzles with other puzzles or in a center with other environmental print games.

◆ VARIATIONS/EXTENSIONS

Depending on the number of boxes available, each child can glue the pieces of the puzzle back together on a piece of paper to take home or display.

◆ PARENT CONNECTION

Show parents how easy it is to use boxes and bags accumulated in daily routines to provide easy puzzles for children to enjoy.

◆ ASSESSMENT

Observe children's ability to complete puzzles and observe whether children can read the label or logo after completing the puzzle.

◆ RELATED LITERATURE, SONGS, AND POEMS

See Resource A.

COUPONS

◆ SUGGESTED GRADE LEVEL

2-3

◆ PURPOSE/RATIONALE

- ◆ Practice mathematical computation
- ◆ Comprehend mathematical language
- ◆ Understand that print has a function

◆ MATERIALS

- ◆ Coupons from newspaper ads, magazines, or mail flyers
- ◆ Paper
- ◆ Glue

◆ PROCEDURE

Have each child choose three coupons. The children then arrange the coupons in order from least to greatest, according to cost. Children glue the coupons, in the correct order, on a sheet of paper.

◆ VARIATIONS/EXTENSIONS

Children can practice addition and subtraction using the cost of the items on the coupons. Children can use the coupons to figure out which items they can purchase when given a specific amount to spend, and they can figure prices of items when the coupon amount is deducted from the original price of the product.

◆ PARENT CONNECTION

Parents can have children help compile a shopping list. Using coupons from newspapers, magazines, and store displays, parents can ask children to figure the amount of discount and the final cost of the product.

◆ ASSESSMENT

Ordered coupons show students' knowledge of mathematical language and computation.

◆ RELATED LITERATURE, SONGS, AND POEMS

Don't Forget the Bacon, by P. Hutchins

GRAPHS

◆ SUGGESTED GRADE LEVEL

PreK–3

◆ PURPOSE/RATIONALE

◆ Participate in graphing and categorizing

◆ MATERIALS

◆ Enlarged graphs
◆ Environmental print provided by children

◆ PROCEDURE

Have the children collect data to graph. For example, children might survey the class to find out the class's favorite fast-food restaurant. Have the children use labels and logos from restaurants to create a graph reflecting the class's response to the survey.

◆ VARIATIONS/EXTENSIONS

Other examples of graphs include favorite animal, cartoon, school subject, ice cream, snack, cereal, chips, colas, and so on.

◆ PARENT CONNECTION

Allow children to survey their own families and friends with questions used in the classroom activities and create graphs reflecting the survey data.

◆ ASSESSMENT

The activity provides evidence of children's understanding of graphs and categorization.

◆ RELATED LITERATURE, SONGS, AND POEMS

See Resource A.

MATH GAMES

◆ SUGGESTED GRADE LEVEL

PreK–2

◆ PURPOSE/RATIONALE

- ◆ Build mathematical concepts
- ◆ See print in varied contexts

◆ MATERIALS

- ◆ Poster board or other materials to make board games
- ◆ Models of familiar card and board games
- ◆ Plastic sandwich bags

◆ PROCEDURE

Using environmental print, make games that are similar to the math games children play in the classroom. For example, for the game bingo, use labels, signs, and logos for each square, instead of numbers or letters. Other games children can make include math versions of tic-tac-toe, lotto, and concentration. See the example for Brand Name Bingo on the next page.

◆ VARIATIONS/EXTENSIONS

For a memory game, make two cards for each logo using two labels. As the year progresses, make a different level of the game by using one label and a copy of the label to match. Finally, use the label and a card with the written or typed label to match.

◆ PARENT CONNECTION

Send games, with accompanying instructions, home in plastic bags for families to play. Be sure to include inexpensive items, such as bottle caps, for game pieces.

◆ ASSESSMENT

Have children record in their math journals the name of the game and the players as well as instructions for how the game is played.

◆ RELATED LITERATURE, SONGS, AND POEMS

See Resource A.

BRAND NAME BINGO!

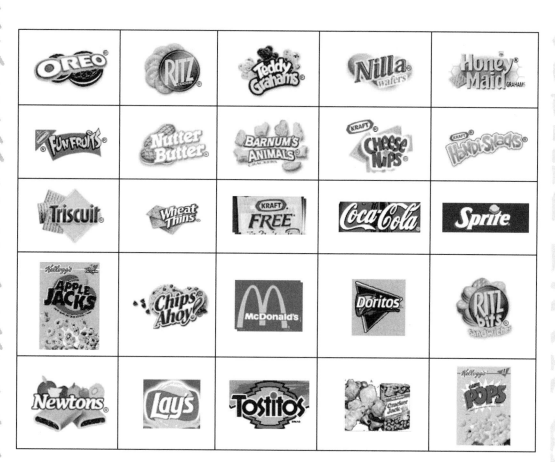

BRAND NAME BINGO!

MATH IN AN INTEGRATED CURRICULUM

◆ SUGGESTED GRADE LEVEL

PreK–2

◆ PURPOSE/RATIONALE

- ◆ Practice one-to-one correspondence

◆ MATERIALS

- ◆ Poster board or other materials needed to make board games
- ◆ Models of familiar card and board games

◆ PROCEDURE

Stories, songs, bulletin boards, class-made books, murals, lists, recipes, and so on can incorporate environmental print labels and logos and be integrated with the math curriculum, for example, by making graphs and playing board games. See the Variations/Extensions section that follows for procedures for specific activities.

◆ VARIATIONS/EXTENSIONS

Insects Lesson

Teach children to play the game "We're Going on a Picnic." Make a picnic basket-shaped game board. Attach labels and logos of things ants might like to eat at a picnic. Have children find the number of products in the basket.

"Me" Lesson

Have each student make a game board in the shape of a child. The game board should be made from sticker dots and children's favorite logos and labels. Have children create rules for their game.

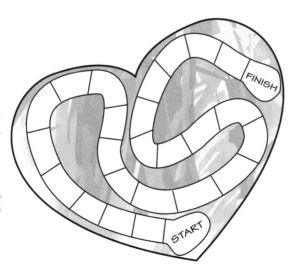

Holidays Lesson

Seasonal game boards, using Christmas tree or Star of David shapes, Valentine shapes, pumpkin shapes, and so on can be made using advertisements from newspapers, catalogs, and magazines. Again, have children create the rules of their self-made game.

MATH IN AN INTEGRATED CURRICULUM

Weather Lesson

Find food, clothing, drinks, machines, and gear used in hot and cold weather. Have the students make classification charts. For example, children's charts might read "Foods we eat in the summer" and "Foods we eat in the winter."

Farm Lesson

Find foods that come from different places on a farm. For example, McDonald's hamburger comes from a cow, and McDonald's French fries come from a plant. Have students make classification charts with headings "Foods that come from animals" and "Foods that come from plants."

Ocean Lesson

Find foods that come from the ocean. Have children create a game using materials and logos gathered from local seafood restaurants.

Transportation Lesson

Have children make a map of community businesses on a game board. Using toy trucks as game pieces, have children deliver product labels and logos to the appropriate businesses.

◆ PARENT CONNECTION

Send game boards, with accompanying playing instructions, home for families to play. Include inexpensive items, such as bottle caps, for game pieces.

◆ ASSESSMENT

Have children record information about the math game, the players, and any scorekeeping in their math journals.

◆ RELATED LITERATURE, SONGS, AND POEMS

Books, songs, and poems used for thematic studies, as well as *Trucks*, by D. Crews, for the transportation lesson.

◆ SUGGESTED GRADE LEVEL

PreK-2

◆ PURPOSE/RATIONALE

- ◆ Define and identify more, less, and equal
- ◆ Make one-to-one correspondences
- ◆ Categorize items
- ◆ See environmental print in varied contexts

◆ MATERIALS

- ◆ Individual serving packets of M&M's candy
- ◆ *The M&M's Counting Book,* by B. McGrath

◆ PROCEDURE

Provide each child with a packet of M&M's. Have the children sort the M&M's by color to count and find out which color they have the most—and least—of in their packet. Ask children to arrange the colors from the least to the greatest.

Read *The M&M's Counting Book* aloud to the class. Have the children count the candies as you read.

◆ VARIATIONS/EXTENSIONS

Skittles or Valentine heart candies can be used also. Be sure to check for any food allergies the children might have before implementing this activity.

◆ PARENT CONNECTION

Host a math night for parents to allow them to experience some of the games and activities used in the classroom. Have parents determine the purpose/rationale for each game. Ask parents to think of other ways to provide children with similar activities at home. Allow parents to check out books from the classroom library.

◆ ASSESSMENT

Have the children record their work and mathematical thinking in their math journals.

◆ RELATED LITERATURE, SONGS, AND POEMS

The M&M's Counting Book, by B. McGrath

FOOD LABELS

◆ SUGGESTED GRADE LEVEL

3

◆ PURPOSE/RATIONALE

- ◆ Practice mathematical computation
- ◆ Identify components of a nutrition label
- ◆ Use functional print

◆ MATERIALS NEEDED

- ◆ Food labels from items served at a meal

◆ PROCEDURE

Have the children bring in food labels from one meal they have eaten. Using the labels, have the children determine the amount of fat grams in the meal they ate.

◆ VARIATIONS/EXTENSIONS

Have children find the total amount of calories consumed in a day. Calculate the amount of ingredients in a meal.

Have children bring in a box or wrapper from their favorite food. Have the children create people using the box or wrapper as a body. Title the display "You Are What You Eat."

◆ PARENT CONNECTION

Have the child record data for the family on caloric intake, fat grams, and so on.

◆ ASSESSMENT

Children can show their computation in a math journal.

◆ RELATED LITERATURE, SONGS, AND POEMS

See Resource A.

ENLARGED CLASS TEXTS

◆ ## SUGGESTED GRADE LEVEL

PreK–2

◆ ## PURPOSE/RATIONALE

- ◆ See environmental print in varied contexts
- ◆ Build fluency

◆ ## MATERIALS NEEDED

- ◆ Poster paper or tagboard
- ◆ Environmental print labels, logos, and signs
- ◆ 12" × 18" construction paper
- ◆ Markers, crayons, and paint
- ◆ Glue

◆ ## PROCEDURE

Select a text that is familiar to the children, such as a song, chant, poem, or book, and have them write the text on a large sheet of poster paper or tagboard. Add environmental print labels where appropriate. Allow the children to add illustrations to their poster pages. Display the poster pages in the room for the children to practice reading. After children have practiced reading, take the pages down and make into a class big book. Reread the book with the class to expose them to words in context and in manuscript or type.

◆ ## VARIATIONS/EXTENSIONS

Variations depend on the variety of books used for language exploration in shared readings.

◆ ## PARENT CONNECTION

Allow children to take home class books to share with their parents.

◆ ## ASSESSMENT

Observe and record literacy and math anecdotal records from children's individual pages.

◆ ## RELATED LITERATURE, SONGS, AND POEMS

Have You Ever Been to Kmart? (song sung to the tune of "Have you Ever Seen a Lassie?")
Eating the Alphabet, by L. Ehlert
On Market Street, by A. Lobel

LISTS

◆ SUGGESTED GRADE LEVEL

1–3

◆ PURPOSE/RATIONALE

- ◆ Complete mathematical computation
- ◆ Create graphs
- ◆ Use mathematical language of more, less, and equal
- ◆ See environmental print in varied contexts

◆ MATERIALS

- ◆ Catalogs
- ◆ Newspaper advertisements from local stores

◆ PROCEDURE

Have children make a Christmas or birthday wish list by cutting out items from newspapers and catalogs. Then, have the children add the total cost of the items on their list.

◆ VARIATIONS/EXTENSIONS

Designate a set amount for each child to spend and have them figure out what they can purchase.

Conduct a class survey to determine children's favorite gifts. Have the children create a graph titled "Top Ten Gifts of Our Class."

◆ PARENT CONNECTION

After determining popular gift items, parents can encourage their children to work to earn money to purchase a gift for another child in need.

Have each family member make a wish list for others to use. They can make several lists for different budgets—for example, gifts under $1, $5, $10, and so on.

◆ ASSESSMENT

Mathematical computation can be recorded in a math journal. Class graphs can be displayed and photographed for evidence of children's work.

◆ RELATED LITERATURE, SONGS, AND POEMS

See Resource A.

GROCERY STORE SURVEYS

◆ SUGGESTED GRADE LEVEL

1-3

◆ PURPOSE/RATIONALE

- ◆ Compile data
- ◆ Use functional print
- ◆ Complete mathematical computations

◆ MATERIALS

- ◆ Prices from various area grocery stores

◆ PROCEDURE

Write down prices of specific items while in the grocery store, or have students or parents write them down and bring the prices to class. Have the students use the prices from grocery stores to compare differences. Ask them to identify which store is least and most expensive.

◆ VARIATIONS/EXTENSIONS

Have students add the items from each store to determine which store has the lowest overall food prices. Display totals on area grocery bags. Have the students check the prices for several weeks and note any changes. The students can also inform area grocery store of their findings.

◆ PARENT CONNECTION

Using advertisements from local stores or newspapers, children can help their parents determine where to find the lowest-priced items.

◆ ASSESSMENT

Have the children record their computation in their math journals.

◆ RELATED LITERATURE, SONGS, AND POEMS

See Resource A.

FOOD GROUPS

◆ SUGGESTED GRADE LEVEL

K-3

◆ PURPOSE/RATIONALE

- ◆ Categorize labels
- ◆ Complete mathematical computations
- ◆ Use functional print

◆ MATERIALS

- ◆ Poster of the Food Pyramid
- ◆ Labels from meals at home or at school
- ◆ Paper
- ◆ Glue

◆ PROCEDURE

Have students collect labels from food items they ate at a meal. Ask students to glue the labels onto a poster of the government's Food Pyramid. Then, have students calculate serving sizes to find out if they ate the daily recommended amount of each food group. Students can chart individual or class results for a week.

◆ VARIATIONS/EXTENSIONS

Using the school menu, have students determine where each food served fits into the Food Pyramid. Ask students, "How do you think the lunchroom manager selects foods to be served each day?" Have the lunchroom manager speak to the class about his or her job. You can also have a nutritionist or dietitian speak to the class.

◆ PARENT CONNECTION

Family members can record in a journal the foods they eat for a week and check nutritional information.

◆ ASSESSMENT

Have students record their mathematical computations in their math journals. Note whether younger children can glue environmental print food items in proper areas of the Food Pyramid.

◆ RELATED LITERATURE, SONGS, AND POEMS

Pigs Will Be Pigs, by A. Axelrod

CHAPTER FOUR

Health and Science Activities

Young children are scientists by nature. They observe processes and how things change. An important way young scientists learn is to discuss what they observe and do. Vygotsky (1978) believed that speech makes all higher thought possible. What that means for young scientists is that they must talk through what they do. Oral language development is the foundation for literacy. For most of the health and science environmental print activities found in this chapter, we encourage you to have students talk through the activities. Remember, speech makes higher thinking possible.

There is an abundance of environmental print that relates to health and science. Signs outside grocery stores, nutrition facts labels on containers, signs and logos inside stores, names of stores on bags and shopping lists, and logos on money, menus, fast-food containers and wrappers, recipes, seed packets, and clothing are continually viewed by children. This environmental print can easily be incorporated into the curriculum through health and science activities. Further, fingerplays and related literature can be used to teach health and science. A good collection of fingerplays related to science and health was compiled by Cromwell and Hibner (1976).

The following environmental print activities can be used for teaching health and science:

MAKING FLAVORED MILK

◆ SUGGESTED GRADE LEVEL

PreK–2

◆ PURPOSE/RATIONALE

- ◆ Use recipes
- ◆ Observe the change process while making flavored milk
- ◆ Follow directions to make a healthy snack

◆ MATERIALS

- ◆ Milk
- ◆ Powdered strawberry and chocolate flavorings
- ◆ Spoons for stirring
- ◆ One glass for each child

◆ PROCEDURE

Have each child pour his or her own milk into a glass. Then, have them mix either strawberry or chocolate into the milk to flavor it. Provide children with a prepared recipe card that tells them how many teaspoons of flavored powder to add to the milk. Use labels from cans to help the children read the recipes.

Assist students in making individual recipe books, encouraging children to use familiar labels and logos. Have each student document (draw) in the book how the powder changed to cake mix (a semisolid).

◆ VARIATIONS/EXTENSIONS

Take the children to a farm to see a real cow and experience milking a cow.

Make a mural depicting the process milk goes through at a dairy before it gets to the supermarket.

Using milk products from the school cafeteria and classroom kitchen or cooking area, glue familiar labels (e.g., milk cartons or ice cream wrappers showing dairy products) on a mural.

◆ PARENT CONNECTION

Encourage parents to work with children in following recipe cards that turn powder ingredients into liquid. Parents can make simple recipe cards for baking a cake. Further, teachers can send simple recipe cards home for parents to use with their children.

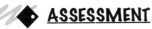

MAKING FLAVORED MILK

◆ ASSESSMENT

Observe students making strawberry or chocolate milk from flavored powder. Check individual recipe books to make sure students are using appropriate logos and documenting the change process.

◆ RELATED LITERATURE, SONGS, AND POEMS

In the Night Kitchen, by M. Sendak
It Looked Like Spilt Milk, by C. Shaw

MAKING FLAVORED MILK

PEANUT BUTTER AND JELLY SANDWICHES

 ## SUGGESTED GRADE LEVEL

PreK–2

 ## PURPOSE/RATIONALE

- ◆ Follow directions
- ◆ Orally describe a process

MATERIALS

- ◆ Plastic knife and spoon
- ◆ Plate or paper towels
- ◆ Napkins
- ◆ Coupons or labels showing recipe items
- ◆ Bread
- ◆ Peanut butter
- ◆ Jelly

 ## PROCEDURE

Make a large recipe card for children to read by using simple words, drawings (measuring utensils), and labels of the foods used in the recipe. For example, for spreading peanut butter and jelly on bread, make the following card:

1 slice of bread (label) + peanut butter (label)
1 slice of bread + jelly (label)

VARIATIONS/EXTENSIONS

Use only peanut butter, or make a coconut and peanut butter sandwich.

 ## PARENT CONNECTION

Continue to encourage parents to help their children follow recipe cards, using environmental print labels. Parents might use recipe cards with their children to make a tomato sandwich, a chicken salad spread, a pimento and cheese, and so on. Sample recipes can be sent home if needed.

ASSESSMENT

Observe students making the peanut butter and jelly sandwiches.

The following simple checklist can be used to evaluate students' oral language. Write comments about each child's explanation of how to make a peanut butter and jelly sandwich.

Oral Language Checklist

Sample: Making a Peanut Butter and Jelly Sandwich		
Beginning Statement	*Middle Statements*	*Ending Statement*

◆ RELATED LITERATURE, SONGS, AND POEMS

Peanut Butter, by A. Erlbach
Peanut Butter and Jelly, by N. B. Westcott

MAKING M&M'S COOKIES

 SUGGESTED GRADE LEVEL

PreK–3

 PURPOSE/RATIONALE

- ◆ Follow simple and complex recipes
- ◆ Orally describe a process
- ◆ Develop fine motor skills
- ◆ Observe how temperature changes the state of matter

◆ **MATERIALS**

- ◆ Recipe written on poster board
- ◆ Cookie sheet
- ◆ Spatula
- ◆ M&M's candies
- ◆ Oven
- ◆ Table knife
- ◆ Roll of sugar cookie dough from grocer's cooler or premixed homemade sugar cookies

 PROCEDURE

Using a half sheet of poster board, write a simple recipe using labels from cookie dough ingredients and M&M's candies. Demonstrate how to cut the cold dough into slices. Supervise as the children cut the dough with a table knife. Suggest that the children decorate the cookie by placing M&M's on the top and bottom. Bake the cookies in oven according to package or recipe directions.

◆ **VARIATIONS/EXTENSIONS**

Children can create their own recipe cards from labels collected from the environmental print box.

◆ **PARENT CONNECTION**

If possible, host a workshop for parents on using environmental print recipes with children. Provide them with sample recipes and assist them in making a recipe book for their children.

Continue to send home examples of environmental print recipes for parents and children to use together. Ask parents to encourage their children to talk through the recipes as they follow them.

ASSESSMENT

Sample oral language development using the following Oral Language Checklist.

Oral Language Checklist

Sample: Making M&M's Cookies		
Beginning Statement	*Middle Statements*	*Ending Statement*

 ## RELATED LITERATURE, SONGS, AND POEMS

"The Easter Kitchen" (poem), by B. Bagert
The M&M's Counting Book, by B. McGrath

MAKING CHICKEN OR VEGETABLE STEW

◆ SUGGESTED GRADE LEVEL

PreK-2

◆ PURPOSE/RATIONALE

- ◆ Discuss and select healthy foods
- ◆ Orally describe a process
- ◆ Follow a recipe

◆ MATERIALS

- ◆ Ingredients for any simple stew recipe (e.g., beef broth, carrots, onions, potatoes)

Or

- ◆ Can of stew
- ◆ Slow cooker
- ◆ Coupons, labels, or pictures that depict stew ingredients
- ◆ Large plastic or wooden spoon for stirring

◆ PROCEDURE

After a discussion concerning good nutrition, allow children to assist in deciding which healthy foods should go in a stew. Purchase items at the grocery store. Make a recipe card for children to follow by using pictures and labels instead of words. Guide the children in mixing the ingredients and stirring the stew as it cooks.

◆ VARIATIONS/EXTENSIONS

After a discussion about good nutrition, children can choose ingredients they think need to go in stew by selecting pictures from the environmental print box and gluing them to a large poster of a pot.

Encourage children to write down what they think goes in chicken stew. Pictures and labels can be used with the print. A class book or recipe file can be compiled for children to take home.

Another variation would be to make vegetarian stew. Have the children brainstorm vegetables they think should be included in a stew that does not contain meat. You can discuss protein and the substitution of beans for meat.

◆ PARENT CONNECTION

Send the recipe home for parents to try. Encourage parents to discuss the process with their children.

◆ ASSESSMENT

Observe students' social interaction while discussing what ingredients should be used in making stew. As a class, make a large chart with the headings "Healthy Foods" and "Unhealthy Foods." After discussing the class chart, interview each child. Say, "Tell me some healthy foods you think would taste good in stew." Then ask, "What are some unhealthy foods that you would not want to put in a stew?"

◆ RELATED LITERATURE, SONGS, AND POEMS

"Carrot Stew" (song), by Disney Co.
Stone Soup, by H. Forrest
Stone Soup, by M. Brown
The Wolf's Chicken Stew, by K. Kasza

MAKING PIZZA

MAKING PIZZA

 ◆ **SUGGESTED GRADE LEVEL**

PreK–2

 ◆ **PURPOSE/RATIONALE**

- ◆ Identify and discuss healthy foods
- ◆ Follow directions

 ◆ **MATERIALS**

- ◆ Canned refrigerator biscuits
- ◆ Pasta sauce
- ◆ Pepperoni slices, chopped
- ◆ Grated mozzarella cheese
- ◆ Oven
- ◆ Cookie sheet
- ◆ Pot holders
- ◆ Spatula
- ◆ Small rolling pin or similar object

 ◆ **PROCEDURE**

Have children wash their hands thoroughly and open the cans of biscuits. Demonstrate for the children how to pat or roll out each biscuit until flattened to about 1/4- to 1/2-inch thickness. Spread pasta sauce on the biscuits and place pepperoni and cheese on top of the sauce. Bake the pizzas in a 400-degree oven for about 5 minutes. While preparing the pizzas, guide the conversation toward the nutritional value of the pizza ingredients.

 ◆ **VARIATIONS/EXTENSIONS**

Each child can make a small 6-inch pizza from a mix. Provide a variety of toppings and let each child create his or her own healthy pizza. You can also provide ingredients for a large pizza and have the children take turns assembling it. Pizza can also be ordered from a take-out restaurant, or the class can visit a pizza restaurant and watch pizza being made.

Children can add the pizza recipe to a recipe book.

 ◆ **PARENT CONNECTION**

Send home the recipe invented by the children for the parents and children to experiment with at home.

MAKING PIZZA

 ### ◆ ASSESSMENT

Observe the students making the pizza, using biscuit dough and the ingredients the students suggested.

Check the individual recipes created by the children.

 ### ◆ RELATED LITERATURE, SONGS, AND POEMS

Pete's a Pizza, by W. Steig

MAKING PIZZA

MAKING PANCAKES

SUGGESTED GRADE LEVEL

PreK–2

PURPOSE/RATIONALE

- Follow directions on a rebus card
- Work collaboratively

MATERIALS

- Pancake mix with required ingredients
- Syrup
- Margarine or butter
- Electric skillet (placed in a cardboard box for safety)
- Spatula

PROCEDURE

Make a large rebus recipe card using labels of the ingredients. Have the children mix the ingredients and cook the pancakes according to the recipe.

VARIATIONS/EXTENSIONS

Read *Pancakes, Pancakes,* by Eric Carle. Have children cut paper into a round pancake shape. Then, have them write their own recipes for various types of pancakes, such as banana pancakes (using environmental print labels for foods they want to use in their pancakes).

PARENT CONNECTION

Send a copy of the rebus recipe cards home. Encourage parents to work with children to follow the recipe cards to make pancakes. Ask parents to point out to children how a powder was turned into a liquid.

ASSESSMENT

Observe the students making pancakes.

See if each child can identify the words used in the recipe (with and without the rebus picture). Ingredients for the checklist include eggs, milk, oil, syrup, and margarine.

RELATED LITERATURE, SONGS, AND POEMS

Pancakes for Breakfast, by T. dePaola
"Round as a Pancake" (song), in *Exploring Music Kindergarten,* by
E. Boardman and B. Landis

PRETEND SHOPPING

 ◆ <u>SUGGESTED GRADE LEVEL</u>

PreK-2

 ◆ <u>PURPOSE/RATIONALE</u>

- ◆ Make a shopping/grocery list
- ◆ Determine the price of an item
- ◆ Count money

 ◆ <u>MATERIALS</u>

- ◆ Coupons
- ◆ Toy cash register
- ◆ Play money
- ◆ Note pads for shopping lists
- ◆ Pencils
- ◆ Empty, clean food containers

 ◆ <u>PROCEDURE</u>

Use either an existing home living area or a corner of the room for this noisy activity. Provide children with coupons for familiar food items; clean, empty food containers of familiar food items; and note pads and pencils for lists. Place the cash register where it is easily accessible to the students.

 ◆ <u>VARIATIONS/EXTENSIONS</u>

Product containers can be used as a three-dimensional bulletin board. Include prices on each item for math reinforcement.

 ◆ <u>PARENT CONNECTION</u>

Ask parents to send in empty food containers to use in the pretend grocery store.

◆ <u>ASSESSMENT</u>

Examine grocery lists made by the children to evaluate their levels of writing.

◆ <u>RELATED LITERATURE, SONGS, AND POEMS</u>

The Berenstain Bears Get the Gimmies, by S. Berenstain and J. Berenstain
  General Store, by R. Field
The Little Old Man Who Could Not Read, by I. S. Black
Matthew Likes to Read, by J. Grainger
"The Pretend Grocery Store" (song), by Raffi
Something Good, by R. Munsch
The Story of Money, by B. Maestro

REAL SHOPPING

◆ SUGGESTED GRADE LEVEL

PreK–2

◆ PURPOSE/RATIONALE

- ◆ Identify items in a grocery store
- ◆ Read a shopping list

◆ MATERIALS

- ◆ Shopping lists
- ◆ Pencils
- ◆ Camera

◆ PROCEDURE

Have children create a shopping list. Secure extra assistance and parental permission to take children to the grocery store. You may find it helpful to notify the grocer that you are coming. Walk through the grocery store in small groups so that the children have an adult available to answer questions. Begin by pointing out to the children the items with which they would be most familiar. They will soon take your lead by showing you items they know. Show them the nutrition facts labels on food items and explain them in a simple manner to children. Let the children find the items on their shopping lists with as little assistance as possible. Allow them to assist in checking out the items. If possible, refer to the government Food Pyramid to determine how food items might be categorized.

NOTE: If children are not purchasing items on their shopping lists, have them check the items on their lists or take pictures of the items while in the store.

◆ VARIATIONS/EXTENSIONS

Let the students plan a snack or meal as appropriate for a thematic study. Let them make a list and go to the store to shop for the items.

◆ PARENT CONNECTION

Ask parents to send a copy of their family's shopping list to class. If possible, have parents volunteer to go on the class shopping trip.

ASSESSMENT

Check the shopping lists created by the students.

Create a class shopping list and have each student read it.

 RELATED LITERATURE, SONGS, AND POEMS

General Store, by R. Field

GOOD FOOD VERSUS JUNK FOOD

◆ **SUGGESTED GRADE LEVEL**

PreK–2

◆ **PURPOSE/RATIONALE**

- ◆ Identify healthy foods
- ◆ Recognize and use the words *good* and *junk* to describe food

◆ **MATERIALS**

- ◆ Drawings or representations of two grocery carts, one labeled "Good Food," one labeled "Junk Food"
- ◆ Glue or tape
- ◆ Pictures of food and food labels

◆ **PROCEDURE**

Research the importance of "good" foods and "junk" foods. Read one or more of the books in the Related Literature section and discuss the differences between good food and junk food. Sort the food labels and pictures and place them on the good grocery cart or the junk grocery cart. This can be done together as an introductory activity.

◆ **VARIATIONS/EXTENSIONS**

Introduce the nutrition facts panel on product labels and discuss the ingredients and contents of foods.

◆ **PARENT CONNECTION**

Ask parents to help their child journal or document the foods they consume at home, using the same activity.

◆ **ASSESSMENT**

Check the finished grocery cart products of each child.

◆ **RELATED LITERATURE, SONGS, AND POEMS**

The Berenstain Bears and Too Much Junk Food, by S. Berenstain and J. Berenstain
The Berenstain Bears Get the Gimmies, by S. Berenstain and J. Berenstain
Something Good, by R. Munsch
There's an Alligator Under My Bed, by M. Mercer

SNACKS—HOW GOOD ARE THEY?

◆ SUGGESTED GRADE LEVEL

PreK–2

◆ PURPOSE

- ◆ Categorize snacks as either "good," "better," or "best"
- ◆ Recognize the superlatives *good*, *better*, and *best* and use them appropriately

◆ MATERIALS

- ◆ Snacks brought to school by the students
- ◆ Large sheet of paper to cover a table

◆ PROCEDURE

Teach the children about nutritious foods. Have the children take out their snacks for the day and evaluate their nutritional value. On the paper-covered table, draw three columns and label them "Good," "Better," and "Best." Have the children decide where their snack best fits and place it in the appropriate column. Help the students determine the percentage of nutritious snacks for the day. This activity can be done for several days so students can note any changes in nutritional values.

◆ VARIATIONS/EXTENSIONS

Hang a large sheet of butcher paper on a wall where the children can paste pictures of "good," "better," and "best" foods. These may be pictures of foods and labels from the environmental print box.

◆ PARENT CONNECTION

Provide parents with ideas for nutritional snacks for their children.

Send a chart home for parents and children to categorize home snacks as "good," "better," and "best."

◆ ASSESSMENT

Check students' placement of foods on the graph. After the entire chart is constructed, have each student read the environmental print and the names of foods in each category.

RELATED LITERATURE, SONGS, AND POEMS

The Berenstain Bears and Too Much Junk Food, by S. Berenstain and
  J. Berenstain
The Berenstain Bears Get the Gimmies, by S. Berenstain and J. Berenstain
Something Good, by R. Munsch
There's an Alligator Under My Bed, by M. Mayer

WHERE DOES FOOD GO?

 ### SUGGESTED GRADE LEVEL

PreK–2

 ### PURPOSE/RATIONALE

- ◆ Identify body parts affected by foods
- ◆ Recognize the words *vitamin, protein,* and *calcium*

 ### MATERIALS

- ◆ Markers
- ◆ Glue or tape
- ◆ Pictures and labels of nutritional foods
- ◆ Butcher paper for drawing outline of a child

 ### PROCEDURE

Draw a large outline of a child on butcher paper. Then, teach the children about vitamins, explaining their function in the different parts of the body. Have the children identify the vitamins represented by foods in various pictures and labels. Then, have them place the pictures and labels on the paper body at a place where the nutrient is needed:

Fruits are needed for body cells.

Vitamin C helps the body fight infections.

Vitamin A from carrots helps the body grow and promotes good eyesight and normal tooth development.

Vitamin B helps cells use oxygen and keeps skin and nerves healthy.

Foods in the bread group provide fiber, which assists the digestive system.

Milk, yogurt, and cheese are sources of protein and calcium, which help bones grow and keep teeth strong.

Protein can come from meats, peanuts, beans, and other sources and helps keep the hair, bones, muscles, teeth, and brain healthy.

 ### VARIATIONS/EXTENSIONS

Provide children with a Nutrient Notebook that contains a different nutrient on top of each page (e.g., for vitamin C, the name and an orange juice label can be at the top of the page). Children can glue pictures and labels onto the pages.

WHERE DOES FOOD GO?

WHERE DOES FOOD GO?

◆ PARENT CONNECTION

Ask parents to send in labels of foods children eat at home.

◆ ASSESSMENT

Check children's placement of pictures and labels to evaluate the appropriate placement.

◆ RELATED LITERATURE, SONGS, AND POEMS

The Berenstain Bears and Too Much Junk Food, by S. Berenstain and J. Berenstain

The Magic School Bus Inside the Human Body, by J. Cole

PRETEND RESTAURANT

◆ **SUGGESTED GRADE LEVEL**

PreK–2

◆ **PURPOSE/RATIONALE**

- ◆ Develop an awareness and appreciation for different types of restaurants
- ◆ Participate in role plays
- ◆ Practice reading environmental print words

◆ **MATERIALS**

- ◆ Items from a fast-food restaurant in your area (e.g., napkins, placemats, cups, containers)
- ◆ Menus made from fast-food restaurant items
- ◆ Pencils and writing pads

◆ **PROCEDURE**

Assist children in preparing a restaurant center that includes a small table that allows two to four children to be seated. Discuss ordering foods at restaurant tables and counters, cafeterias, and drive-through windows. Allow for independent planning. Have children pretend to take and give orders in a restaurant, using the props in the restaurant center.

This activity also provides an opportunity for students to play restaurant with foods from various cultures. Periodically and consistently change the type of restaurant. Be sure to include Mexican, Chinese, Thai, Persian, Korean, and other ethnic restaurants located in the neighborhood.

◆ **VARIATIONS/EXTENSIONS**

Encourage different individuals, such as the principal or older peers, to come to the room to place their orders for meals.

◆ **PARENT CONNECTION**

Ask parents to collect and send to class menus from restaurants that provide free copies of menus.

◆ **ASSESSMENT**

Check and discuss the orders taken by the "waiters."
Have students read the environmental print words they know from selected menus.

MATCHING TOOTHPASTE

◆ SUGGESTED GRADE LEVEL

PreK–2

◆ PURPOSE/RATIONALE

◆ Recognize words on toothpaste tubes (e.g., Crest, Colgate, Aim, Pepsodent)
◆ Match toothpaste logos to toothpaste words written in standard manuscript
◆ Create patterns using toothpaste words

◆ MATERIALS

◆ Poster board
◆ Two toothpaste boxes for each brand of toothpaste

◆ PROCEDURE

After a discussion on dental hygiene, use a teacher-made game such as bingo, using familiar toothpaste labels and logos.

Students can also play an ordering game. Show logos of various toothpastes and have the children write the logos in the order shown in standard manuscript.

◆ VARIATIONS/EXTENSIONS

Make similar games with other items used in the home, such as shampoo, soap, or detergent.

◆ PARENT CONNECTION

Ask parents to send in toothpaste boxes from home.

◆ ASSESSMENT

Observe children matching the correct word in manuscript form to the logo. Evaluate the patterns used in the ordering game.

◆ RELATED LITERATURE, SONGS, AND POEMS

"Brush Your Teeth" (song), by Raffi

PLANTING SEEDS

 SUGGESTED GRADE LEVEL

PreK–2

 PURPOSE/RATIONALE:

- ◆ Follow directions to plant seeds
- ◆ Write in journals to document plant growth

 MATERIALS

- ◆ Packages of seeds
- ◆ Spade or spoon
- ◆ Soil
- ◆ Watering can
- ◆ Pots or cups for planting or outdoor garden space

 PROCEDURE

Provide seed packets for the children to view before planting. Ask the children to look at packages and read any labels they can. Then, have them plant the seeds and water them each day. Children should observe their plants each day and record the results of planting in their journals. The effects of sun, water, and soil on plant growth can be observed by placing plants in differing environments (i.e., dark closet vs. bright sunlight).

 VARIATIONS/EXTENSIONS

Students can graph and illustrate the growth of their plants as a class project.

Students can discuss the nutritional value of plants.

Students can make a book of empty seed packets.

 PARENT CONNECTION

Ask parents to donate a package of seeds for the class garden.

Encourage parents to plant seeds and discuss plant growth with their children at home.

 ASSESSMENT

Check the children's journals to make sure the students are documenting plant growth appropriately.

PLANTING SEEDS

 ## RELATED LITERATURE, SONGS, AND POEMS

"Birdseed" (poem), by B. Bagert

The Celebration, by J. Warren

Jack's Garden, by H. Cole

More Piggy Back Songs, by J. Warren

Mother Nature's Gift, by J. Warren

"The Seed" and "The Garden Song" (songs), by J. Warren

"Seeds" (song sung to the tune "Twinkle, Twinkle Little Star"), by J. Walters

"The Seeds Grow" (song sung to the tune of "The Farmer in the Dell"), by J. Walters

SUGGESTED GRADE LEVEL

PreK–2

PURPOSE/RATIONALE

- Develop problem-solving skills
- Demonstrate spatial reasoning
- Reproduce geometric shapes

MATERIALS

- Cardboard food containers
- Food signs

PROCEDURE

Make cars and trucks from various food containers and use them in the home living area.

VARIATIONS/EXTENSIONS

Use other containers, such as cereal boxes, for portfolios for children's work.

Large and small containers of the same product can be used to compare sizes (e.g., big, bigger, and biggest).

PARENT CONNECTION

Ask parents to send in boxes and other food containers from home.

ASSESSMENT

Evaluate completed cars and trucks to be sure students can identify geometric shapes.

The first construction of the cars and trucks can be used as model from which to improve the second iteration.

RELATED LITERATURE, SONGS, AND POEMS

Freight Train, by D. Crews
I Read Signs, by T. Hoban
I Read Symbols, by T. Hoban
The Magic School Bus Inside the Earth, by J. Cole
The Magic School Bus Inside the Human Body, by J. Cole
The Magic School Bus Lost Inside the Solar System, by J. Cole
School Bus, by D. Crews
Truck, by D. Crews
"Wheels on the Bus" (song), by Raffi

WEATHER SYMBOLS

◆ **SUGGESTED GRADE LEVEL**

PreK–2

◆ **PURPOSE/RATIONALE**

◆ Recognize and use weather symbols using a daily weather chart

◆ **MATERIALS**

◆ Newspaper
◆ Weather chart for daily use
◆ Videotape of a television weather report

◆ **PROCEDURE**

Show the children a weather chart during group or circle time and explain the weather symbols. Show a videotape of a television weather report to familiarize the children with weather symbols. Discuss a weather map in the local newspaper. Let the children select the weather symbols needed to record the weather of the day.

◆ **VARIATIONS/EXTENSIONS**

Have the children plot or graph the high or low temperature for a period of time.

◆ **PARENT CONNECTION**

Ask parents to call attention to the weather report on the local news or send in weather maps from the newspaper.

◆ **ASSESSMENT**

Check the completed weather chart each day.

◆ **RELATED LITERATURE, SONGS, AND POEMS**

The Cloud Book, by T. DePaola
"The Cloud Song" (song) Vol. 4, by E. Boardman
"Hawaiian Rainbows" (song) Vol. 4, by E. Boardman
"It's Raining" (song), by P. C. Beall
"Make a Snowman" (song sung to the tune of "Three Blind Mice"), by C. Walters
"Rain, Rain Falling Down" (song sung to the tune of "Row, Row, Row Your Boat"), by J. Warren
"Sing a Rainbow" (song) Vol. 4, by E. Boardman
"Weather Song" (song sung to the tune of "Bingo"), by J. Warren
"Wind Is Blowing" (song sung to the tune of "Are You Sleeping"), by C. Walters

GOING ON A PICNIC

 SUGGESTED GRADE LEVEL

PreK–2

 PURPOSE/RATIONALE

◆ Identify foods necessary for a balanced meal
◆ Categorize foods
◆ Read environmental print labels of self-selected foods

 MATERIALS

◆ Construction paper
◆ Glue or paste
◆ Labels and logos of picnic items

 PROCEDURE

Have the children trace and cut out a picnic basket shape from tagboard or construction paper. Discuss with children appropriate, nutritional foods for a picnic. Have the children select food labels of foods they would like to take on a picnic and glue or paste the labels onto their baskets.

 VARIATIONS/EXTENSIONS

Take the children to the store to purchase items for a real picnic.

Go on a real picnic.

Pack a lunchbox (similar to picnic basket).

 PARENT CONNECTION

Ask the parents to plan a family picnic.

 ASSESSMENT

Evaluate the children's choices in their completed picnic basket.

 RELATED LITERATURE, SONGS, AND POEMS

Peanut Butter and Jelly, by N. Westcott
Something Good, by R. Munsch

CHAPTER FIVE

Social Studies Activities

Many teachers tell us that they spend so much time on the literacy and math curricula that there is little time for social studies. In a traditional classroom, we might agree. However, a classroom that is a print-rich environment can naturally incorporate an incredible amount of social science activities. Marie Clay (1993) found that children explore the details of print in their environment, on signs, cereal packages, and television advertisements. They also explore newspapers, postcards, maps, and magazines as they travel in the car with their families. For low-income children, we can provide these print forms that bring social studies to life.

Social studies is more important in early childhood education than ever before. With the passage of the No Child Left Behind Act, social studies has taken a backseat to math, reading, and writing. Teachers tell us that they no longer teach social science because it is not tested on standardized tests. Even though most preschool, kindergarten, and primary-level children will hopefully have little experience with standardized tests, teachers of young children are still reluctant to teach social studies because literacy and math objectives take up most of the day.

Shapiro and Mitchell (1992) explained that "every child, every person, is a part of a number of communities—family (or families), neighborhood(s), cultural and ethnic group(s)" (p. 19). To function in a democratic society, young children must learn to be members of a group, tolerate differences of opinion, and engage in various types of interactions with people. As the communities children live in become more diverse, it is vital to include social studies as a major part of the early childhood curriculum.

The academic curriculum is being pushed down into preschool, but young children experiencing this push often lack the social interactions necessary to get along with others. As we mentioned earlier, environmental print can serve as a bridge between home and school and the larger community. Environmental print can be used extensively through social studies to help build a sense of community and encourage young learners to become active, participating, and negotiating members of the class and society.

We provide many activities for using environmental print in social studies:

USING THE NEWSPAPER

 ## SUGGESTED GRADE LEVEL

2–3

 ## PURPOSE/RATIONALE

◆ Use the newspaper for authentic reading and writing, math computation, and classification

MATERIALS

◆ Local newspapers (preferably one for every child)
◆ Newsprint
◆ Glue or paste
◆ Pencils, pens, and markers
◆ Desktop publishing program

 ## PROCEDURE

Have the newspaper delivered to your room every day. If this is not possible, bring your own newspaper from home and share it. (Some newspapers provide discounts for classrooms.) Introduce each section of the newspaper and have groups of students report a section of the news. Students can develop a classroom newspaper, patterned after the local newspaper. Again, groups can be responsible for gathering and printing news from their chosen section.

In many newspapers, the Wednesday and Sunday editions have large advertisement sections. Have students compare and contrast the sales and prices of various stores. Students can also compare the numbers of clothing advertisements versus the number of car advertisements. (See *The Story of Money* in Resource A.)

Students can also paraphrase the news. This may be difficult for some second graders. However, children in higher grades or those with higher reading abilities can scaffold students who have difficulty reading and paraphrasing the news. For another reading activity, have students read a lead story, sports story, or another article and create a web for it. Or students can invent their own way to represent a news article.

Provide continuity in using the newspaper by promoting record keeping about the news. One good example of this is the weather report. Children can keep a daily record (from the newspaper) of high and low temperatures for the month and then make a graph or determine the mean temperature of

USING THE NEWSPAPER

the city for the month. Other sections of the news lend themselves to record keeping, such as the sports section, the editorial section, and even the want ads.

Students can be asked to think of ways to classify the news they read. For example, they may wish to work in groups to keep up with local, state, national, or even international news. You can extend the news through oral language by having children report the news as TV anchors. Perhaps the helper for the day or week could serve as the anchorperson.

◆ VARIATIONS/EXTENSIONS

Have students extend the news by researching areas from the paper that are of interest to them. Some students may choose to find out more about elections during the month of November. Other students may choose to interview their parents, grandparents, or neighbors about their opinions or the news.

Have the students vote on issues of interest in the newspaper. All areas of the newspaper can be used for some type of voting. If there is a ball game of interest to many, have the students vote on which team they think will win. Students can vote on their favorite section of the newspaper, their favorite comic strip, their favorite sports team, and so on.

Have students record their own news and the headline news in a newspaper journal. Place the journals in a newspaper literacy center to encourage independent work.

◆ PARENT CONNECTION

Send newspapers home with the children. Parents and children can read the newspaper together and discuss it or together complete many of the authentic tasks described in the previous sections.

◆ ASSESSMENT

Assessment for using the newspaper takes many forms, depending on the newspaper activity completed. Work with students to edit the classroom newspaper, evaluating their language skills. Check students' paraphrased news articles to see if they include all of the important events or news. Observe the daily record keeping of the high and low temperatures for a particular month of the year. Read the news classification of each group (i.e., the local, state, national, and international news). Videotape the news anchor of the day and discuss the strengths and weaknesses of the anchor's reporting and information accuracy.

USING THE NEWSPAPER

◆ RELATED LITERATURE, SONGS, AND POEMS

The Cloud Book, by T. dePaola
Everything from a Nail to a Coffin, by I. Van Rynbach
People, People, Everywhere!, by N. Van Laan

Using just the newspaper provides many
social studies experiences.

POSTCARD TRAVEL

 ### SUGGESTED GRADE LEVEL

K-3

 ### PURPOSE/RATIONALE

◆ "Map" and discuss places friends and relatives have visited

 ### MATERIALS

◆ Bulletin board or display board
◆ Postcards from friends and family

 ### PROCEDURE

Some students will have relatives or friends take trips during the school year. Encourage them to elicit postcards from their friends and relatives. These postcards can be displayed on a map of the United States or world to show where the friends and relatives traveled.

For low-income students and schools, children will rarely have postcards from traveling friends and family. However, this activity can still be used. In such cases, elicit postcards from your own friends and family and from community leaders. We have seen teacher successfully attain postcards in several schools in large urban areas where we teach.

 ### VARIATIONS/EXTENSIONS

If students choose, they can research the places their friends and relatives visited. For example, if a friend sends a postcard from Arizona (see *Arthur's Family Vacation, Messages in the Mailbox,* and *The Jolly Postman* in Resource A), the student might want to find out more about the desert or the Grand Canyon.

 ### PARENT CONNECTION

Send a note home encouraging parents to ask their friends and relatives to send postcards to their home or to the school.

 ### ASSESSMENT

Use your social studies objectives to help elicit postcards. For example, in many states, state history is taught in fourth grade. Encourage postcards from within the state to display and discuss.

POSTCARD TRAVEL

◆ RELATED LITERATURE, SONGS, AND POEMS

Hello Mudduh, Hello Fadduh!, by A. Sherman
The Jolly Christmas Postman, by J. Ahlbert and A. Ahlbert
The Jolly Postman, by J. Ahlbert and A. Ahlbert
A Letter to Amy, by E. J. Keats
Message in the Mailbox, by L. Leedy
My Teacher Sleeps in School, by L. Weiss
There's an Alligator Under My Bed, by M. Mayer
Toddlecreek Post Office, by U. Shulevitz

MAPPING THE COMMUNITY

 SUGGESTED GRADE LEVEL

PreK–2

 PURPOSE/RATIONALE

◆ Use prior knowledge to represent the classroom and community, develop vocabulary, and follow directions

MATERIALS

◆ Poster board or butcher paper
◆ Markers, pencils
◆ Logos and labels from the local community

PROCEDURE

Young children have great difficulty with geographic space. However, maps can still be used in developmentally appropriate ways, if they begin with a classroom map. Have students make a map of the classroom, labeling the parts of the classroom on the map. Then, students can draw a map of how they get to school. This will take time and help, but many students enjoy mapping their route from home to school. Have students identify and record all of the road signs, billboards, and other environmental print they encounter on their way to school.

VARIATIONS/EXTENSIONS

Have students make a map of their own home or dwelling. Students can also draw their house and paste environmental print labels in the rooms of their houses. For example, a student might paste a Tide label in the laundry room or bubble bath in the bathroom.

Take pictures of local buildings and merchants with the environmental print exposed (see *Taxi; People, People, Everywhere; On Market Street; General Store;* and *Everything from a Nail to a Coffin* in Resource A). Students can use the pictures to make a map of the neighborhood.

On field trips, have students record the signs, billboards, and environmental print they encounter during the field trip. Discuss the print at length during sharing time.

PARENT CONNECTION

Send the maps home and ask parents to comment on them.

MAPPING THE COMMUNITY

 ### ◆ ASSESSMENT

The maps children draw can be one "snapshot" for their portfolios. As the class revisits the neighborhood throughout the year, other maps can be added.

Develop a matching game in which logos have been removed from a map of the community. Photocopy the matching game for each student. Have students match the correct label to the right building. Use standard manuscript labels to see if students can read standard manuscript labels.

 ### ◆ RELATED LITERATURE, SONGS, AND POEMS

General Store, by R. Field
I Read Signs, by T. Hoban
I Read Symbols, by T. Hoban
On Market Street, by A. Lobel

COMMUNITY HELPERS

 SUGGESTED GRADE LEVEL

PreK–2

 PURPOSE/RATIONALE

- ◆ Use environmental print to enhance the study of community helpers
- ◆ Write and keep records of familiar logos

 MATERIALS

- ◆ Poster board or butcher paper
- ◆ Markers, pencils
- ◆ Paper

 PROCEDURE

There is hardly an early childhood classroom that does not study community helpers. However, few use environmental print to help in this study. To incorporate print with a study of community helpers, you can have the students write letters, inviting community helpers to visit the class. Follow up the visit by having students write thank-you notes to the guests.

Ask community helpers to bring environmental print related to their particular jobs. Have them share the print during their visit (see *The Signmaker's Assistant, Freight Train, Truck, Parade, I Read Signs, I Read Symbols,* and *My Teacher Sleeps in School* in Resource A). Students can make welcome signs or billboards for the visiting community helpers. Encourage students to be creative with their signs. For example, students can make welcome signs for a policeman in the form of a police badge or police car.

 VARIATIONS/EXTENSIONS

Encourage students to keep a record of all visiting community helpers. They can then make a class or individual community helper book.

Classifying types of merchants and services in the community is a powerful learning experience. Students can classify the types of restaurants, gas stations, grocery stores, banks, tire stores, and so on.

 PARENT CONNECTION

Parents may have community service jobs or jobs of interest and can visit the class to share their expertise.

COMMUNITY HELPERS

 ### <u>ASSESSMENT</u>

Interviews, records, and classification activities can be placed in students' portfolios.

 ### <u>RELATED LITERATURE, SONGS, AND POEMS</u>

The Jolly Postman, by J. Ahlbert and A. Ahlbert
The Jolly Christmas Postman, by J. Ahlbert and A. Ahlbert
The Signmaker's Assistant, by T. Arnold
My Teacher Sleeps in School, by L. Weiss

TRANSPORTATION SCHEDULES

◆ SUGGESTED GRADE LEVEL

2-3

◆ PURPOSE/RATIONALE

- ◆ Plan ahead
- ◆ Identify time zones
- ◆ Understand distances, such as miles and kilometers

◆ MATERIALS

- ◆ Transportation schedules and prices

◆ PROCEDURE

Students can compare transportation types and prices. If possible, invite a local travel agent to class to discuss transportation schedules and costs.

◆ VARIATIONS/EXTENSIONS

Students can plan vacation travel, within a given budget and time frame (depending on their developmental levels).

◆ PARENT CONNECTION

Send travel schedules home and encourage parents to discuss schedules and prices. If parents have access to the Internet, encourage them to compare travel prices to a specific destination using Internet travel sites such as Travelocity.com, Expedia.com, Orbitz.com, and Priceline.com.

◆ ASSESSMENT

Use kidwatching and anecdotal notes to record discussions and plan future experiences with transportation schedules.

NOTE: *Kidwatching* is a term created by Yetta Goodman to denote observing children and recording what they are doing in their natural environment.

◆ RELATED LITERATURE, SONGS, AND POEMS

Arthur's Family Vacation, by M. Arthur
Freight Train, by D. Crews
My Family Vacation, by D. K. Khalsa
School Bus, by D. Crews
Truck, by D. Crews

HOME SALES AND RENTALS

◆ SUGGESTED GRADE LEVEL

2-3

◆ PURPOSE/RATIONALE

◆ Compare prices of houses and apartments in different parts of their community

◆ MATERIALS

◆ Advertisements of homes for sale
◆ Advertisements of apartments for rent

◆ PROCEDURE

Students in the process of moving from one house to another might be interested in looking at homes for sale or apartments for rent. Many communities have free pamphlets describing houses for sale and apartments for rent. Students can compare sections of the city and discuss why prices are different from one section to another.

◆ VARIATIONS/EXTENSIONS

Advanced students might conduct research to find out how homes are financed (see *The Story of Money* in Resource A).

◆ PARENT CONNECTION

Ask parents to send in brochures and other advertising material related to homes for sale and apartments for rent.

◆ ASSESSMENT

Use kidwatching and anecdotal records.

◆ RELATED LITERATURE, SONGS, AND POEMS

Dear Garbage Man, by G. Zion
Jack's Garden, by H. Cole
My Street's a Morning Cool Street, by I. Thomas
My Teacher Sleeps in School, by L. Weiss

ENVIRONMENTAL PRINT GRAPHS AND ELECTIONS

◆ SUGGESTED GRADE LEVEL

PreK–3

◆ PURPOSE/RATIONALE

- ◆ Experience democracy through voting
- ◆ Create graphs of favorite environmental print items

◆ MATERIALS

- ◆ An issue to vote on or a choice to make
- ◆ Overhead or chalkboard to record or graph results

◆ PROCEDURE

As has already been mentioned, all areas of social studies can be graphed. Students can graph their "favorite" of anything studied, from newspaper items for younger children, to the number of children who identify as Republicans or Democrats in the older grades. Some students may conduct follow-up interviews with other students to determine the reasons for their preferences. Even this can be graphed! For example, during the interviews, it might be discovered that seven children voted Democrat in a mock election. Three of the children voted this way because their parents vote Democrat, two voted this way because they simply like the candidate, and two don't know why they voted Democrat.

◆ VARIATIONS/EXTENSIONS

Having a class election, or following a local election, can involve a large amount of print in the environment. Students can make their own election signs, advertisements, and flyers for the candidates. Students may participate in their own election campaigns by giving speeches, explaining why others should vote for them.

◆ PARENT CONNECTION

Ask parents for their opinions on safe topics on which to vote, such as their favorite color.

◆ ASSESSMENT

Students' individual graphs can serve as an assessment. Have each child explain her or his graph.

◆ RELATED LITERATURE, SONGS, AND POEMS

Teddy Bears Go Shopping, by S. Gretz
We Keep a Store, by A. Shelby

CAREERS AND ENVIRONMENTAL PRINT

 ◆ <u>**SUGGESTED GRADE LEVEL**</u>

PreK–1

 ◆ <u>**PURPOSE/RATIONALE**</u>

- ◆ Use functional print
- ◆ Use print in familiar contexts

 ◆ <u>**MATERIALS**</u>

- ◆ Environmental print from the various professions (e.g., magazines for a doctor's office, registration and appointment books, record books and charts)

 ◆ <u>**PROCEDURE**</u>

Allow students to role-play a profession in a specified area of the classroom. Provide books that depict diverse people in different professions, placing them in the area where students are role-playing.

 ◆ <u>**VARIATIONS/EXTENSIONS**</u>

Ask parents and community members who work to speak to the class about their job. Ask them to bring in examples of print they might use on a regular basis.

Before parents arrive, compose a list of questions the students would like to ask the speaker. After the speaker finishes, debrief with the students to see what they learned. List their learning on a language experience chart.

◆ <u>**PARENT CONNECTION**</u>

Ask parents to send in a photograph of them at work. Allow children to document information from these photographs.

◆ <u>**ASSESSMENT**</u>

Evaluate the class graph and language experience chart to find out how much students learned from the guest speakers.

◆ <u>**RELATED LITERATURE, SONGS, AND POEMS**</u>

Harriet Reads Signs and More Signs, by B. Maestro and G. Maestro
Pet Show, by E. J. Keats

SOCIAL STUDIES "ME BOOKS" AND JOURNALS

◆ **SUGGESTED GRADE LEVEL**

K-3

◆ **PURPOSE/RATIONALE**

- ◆ Participate in self-assessment
- ◆ Document learning
- ◆ Understand functionality of print

◆ **MATERIALS**

- ◆ Photographs, maps, postcards, souvenirs, artifacts, realia, and other print resources

◆ **PROCEDURE**

Social studies can be individualized using "Me Books." To create "Me Books," students use scrapbooks, diaries of trips, graphs, research journals, dialogue journals, and other individual print records of what they are studying in social studies. They might also include a list of questions they have generated from discussions and records of what they have found.

◆ **VARIATIONS/EXTENSIONS**

This activity can also be completed as a whole-class activity, documenting the activities and experiences of the class during the school year.

◆ **PARENT CONNECTION**

Ask parents to contribute any items that their child can use in the "Me Book."

◆ **ASSESSMENT**

Evaluate students' finished products.

◆ **RELATED LITERATURE, SONGS, AND POEMS**

Harriet Reads Signs and More Signs, by B. Maestro and G. Maestro
I Read Signs, by T. Hoban
I Read Symbols, by T. Hoban
I Started School Today, by K. G. Frandsen
My Family Vacation, by D. K. Khalsa
My Teacher Sleeps in School, by L. Weiss

CULTURALLY DIVERSE ENVIRONMENTAL PRINT

 ## ◆ <u>SUGGESTED GRADE LEVEL</u>

K–3

 ## ◆ <u>PURPOSE/RATIONALE</u>

- ◆ Build acceptance of, and familiarity with, the various cultures in the community

 ## ◆ <u>MATERIALS</u>

- ◆ Environmental print in other languages of the community

 ## ◆ <u>PROCEDURE</u>

This activity lends itself to many forms of research. For example, children might choose to read and research folktales from different cultures after collecting multicultural environmental print.

 ## ◆ <u>VARIATIONS/EXTENSIONS</u>

Use print from various cultures in the activities described in this book.

 ## ◆ <u>PARENT CONNECTION</u>

Invite parents to share print from their home and communities by sending it to the classroom.

 ## ◆ <u>ASSESSMENT</u>

Evaluate students on their participation in the activities.

 ## ◆ <u>RELATED LITERATURE, SONGS, AND POEMS</u>

On Market Street, by A. Lobel
Pizza for Breakfast, by M. Kovalski

The possibilities for environmental print in social studies are boundless. Using these suggestions as a starter, think of many other ways to use print authentically in the social studies curriculum.

CHAPTER SIX

Creative Dramatics, Music, And Art Activities

The curriculum would not be complete without integrating environmental print in art, music, and drama. Print-enriched play supported by adults using environmental print increases children's aesthetic development (Kuby & Aldridge, 1997; Kuby et al., 1994). This chapter includes some ways to use environmental print to enhance aesthetic growth:

ART COLLAGE

ART COLLAGE

 ## SUGGESTED GRADE LEVEL

PreK–1

 ## PURPOSE/RATIONALE

- ◆ Blend color and design
- ◆ Read familiar labels

 ## MATERIALS

- ◆ Magazines
- ◆ 11- × 14-inch paper
- ◆ Glue
- ◆ Scissors
- ◆ Environmental print
- ◆ Paper

 ## PROCEDURE

Have children cut pictures and logos from magazines, classifying the foods, restaurants, grocery stores, and other items according to their likes and dislikes. Then, have the children create a collage with the pictures and logos.

 ## VARIATIONS/EXTENSIONS

A chart showing different categories can be drawn on each sheet of paper and placed on a wall for continual viewing. The children can add environmental print as it is acquired.

 ## PARENT CONNECTION

Parents can reinforce the lesson with a discussion about the categories of print in the environment.

 ## ASSESSMENT

Observe children to determine whether they can read the print they place in the collage.

RELATED LITERATURE, SONGS, AND POEMS

Eating Up Gladys, by M. Zemach
Something Good, by R. Munsch

STUDYING ARTISTS

◆ SUGGESTED GRADE LEVEL

K-3

◆ PURPOSE/RATIONALE

- ◆ Study artists who use environmental print, such as Norman Rockwell, Jerry Pallotta, and Barbara McGrath

◆ MATERIALS

- ◆ Library books that include environmental print

◆ PROCEDURE

Collect literature for the children to explore and evaluate. Some suggestions are listed in Resource A.

◆ VARIATIONS/EXTENSIONS

Students can become environmental print artists by drawing or painting their own print-rich environments.

◆ PARENT CONNECTION

Have parents reinforce the lesson by providing additional books that contain environmental print (see Resource A).

◆ ASSESSMENT

Have children identify environmental print in their classroom library.

◆ RELATED LITERATURE, SONGS, AND POEMS

The M&M's Counting Book, by B. McGrath
The Spice Alphabet Book, by J. Pallotta

NEIGHBORHOOD MURAL

◆ **SUGGESTED GRADE LEVEL**

2–3

◆ **PURPOSE/RATIONALE**

- ◆ Explore the local neighborhood
- ◆ Identify print in the community

◆ **MATERIALS**

- ◆ Various types and colors of paper
- ◆ Long sheet of butcher paper
- ◆ Glue
- ◆ Markers, crayons, and paints

◆ **PROCEDURE**

Choose a large wall area on which to place the mural. Take the students on a walk to examine the neighborhood and the print on neighborhood buildings and signs. After children return, have the students suggest how to divide up the sections of the mural. Then, have students work to create a mural of the neighborhood. Environmental print for the mural can be taken from the environmental print storage box or brought in from home.

◆ **VARIATIONS/EXTENSIONS**

If a large classroom mural is not possible, a smaller version could be made on a large sheet of paper. Students can complete the mural in school or at home. Have students include their own street in the mural.

◆ **PARENT CONNECTION**

Parents can help collect logos or take their child on a tour of the neighborhood to examine the environmental print.

◆ **ASSESSMENT**

Ask the students to identify the logos in their neighborhood.

◆ **RELATED LITERATURE, SONGS, AND POEMS**

The Bus for Us, by S. Bloom
A Letter to Amy, by E. J. Keats
The Signmaker's Assistant, by T. Arnold

NEIGHBORHOOD MURAL

ME BOXES AND "MYSELF"

◆ **SUGGESTED GRADE LEVEL**

K-1

◆ **PURPOSE/RATIONALE**

- ◆ View and read environmental print
- ◆ Develop vocabulary through discussion

◆ **MATERIALS**

- ◆ A storage box, similar to a pencil box (one per child), for students' environmental print
- ◆ Glue
- ◆ Scissors
- ◆ Markers
- ◆ Butcher paper

◆ **PROCEDURE**

Have the students share with the class the environmental print they brought from home and placed in their boxes. Trace around each child on butcher paper. Have children glue logos from their boxes onto their outline. On the back of their traced bodies, have the children write about the print they brought, describing their experiences with it.

◆ **VARIATIONS/EXTENSIONS**

Talk about nutrition and healthy foods with the class. Then, have the children place pictures of healthy foods onto their outlines.

◆ **PARENT CONNECTION**

Parents can assist in collecting and reading environmental print. They can also discuss healthy food choices with their children.

◆ **ASSESSMENT**

Ask the children to read the environmental print. Observe whether they assist their peers in reading print. Evaluate the healthy-food outlines to determine whether students can choose and identify foods.

◆ **RELATED LITERATURE, SONGS, AND POEMS**

An Alphabet Salad: Fruits and Vegetables from A to Z, by S. L. Schuette
The Berenstain Bears and Too Much Junk Food, by S. Berenstain and
   J. Berenstain

DELIVERY VEHICLES

 ## SUGGESTED GRADE LEVEL

K-1

 ## PURPOSE/RATIONALE

- ◆ Identify names of vehicles

 ## MATERIALS

- ◆ Construction paper
- ◆ Large sheet of butcher paper
- ◆ Magazines and newspapers
- ◆ Scissors
- ◆ Markers, crayons, and pencils

 ## PROCEDURE

Have the children draw trucks, cars, airplanes, vans, and trains onto construction paper and cut them out. Then, have the children write the names of the vehicle's manufacturing company on the picture. Finally, have the children glue their vehicles onto a larger sheet of paper.

 ## VARIATIONS/EXTENSIONS

Have the children create a mural depicting a street scene with delivery vehicles.

 ## PARENT CONNECTION

Provide magazines and newspapers that include photos of vehicles for the children to view and discuss with their parents.

ASSESSMENT

Observe students to determine whether they can match the name of the vehicle manufacturer to the appropriate vehicle. Listen to the children to find out if they can read the names.

RELATED LITERATURE, SONGS, AND POEMS

Truck, by D. Crews
The Wheels on the Bus, by P. Zelinsky

MUSIC—SONGS FOR COMMERCIALS

◆ **SUGGESTED GRADE LEVEL**

K-3

◆ **PURPOSE/RATIONALE**

◆ Develop oral language fluency through music

◆ **MATERIALS**

◆ Logos of businesses included in the jingles

◆ **PROCEDURE**

Have students invent jingles to advertise their favorite products.

◆ **VARIATIONS/EXTENSIONS**

Have student create different lyrics to the same tune, advertising the stores in the community.

◆ **PARENT CONNECTION**

Provide parents with written copies of the children's songs, so the families can sing the jingles together as they drive past businesses in the community.

◆ **ASSESSMENT**

Listen to students' songs and evaluate the lyrics they created.

◆ **RELATED LITERATURE, SONGS, AND POEMS**

The following songs can be used to help the children get started creating their own lyrics:

1. "Did You Ever Go to Kmart?" The class can sing "a tour" of neighborhood franchises to the tune of "Did You Ever See a Lassie?":

> *Did you ever go to Kmart, to Kmart, to Kmart?*
> *Did you ever go to Kmart and what did you see?*

Each student responds, and then the class sings the answer. For example, if a student responds with "a bicycle," the class then would sing:

A bicycle, a bicycle, a bicycle, a bicycle.
Did you ever go to Kmart and what did you see?

The next student responds and the process continues.

2. "A Shopping We Will Go." The song "A Hunting We Will Go" serves as the tune for this song:

A shopping we will go, a shopping we will go,
We look for bargains when we shop, a shopping we will go.
First we'll go to Sears. First we'll go to Sears.
We look for bargains when we shop, and first we'll go to Sears.

Then we'll go to _____, then we'll to _____,
We look for bargains when we shop, and then we'll go to _____.

3. "This Is Hardees." This song is sung to the tune "Are You Sleeping?":

This is Hardees, this is Hardees,
Starts with H, starts with H.
Hamburgers and French fries, hamburgers and French fries,
Mm mm good, mm mm good.

This is Wal-Mart, this is Wal-Mart,
Starts with W, starts with W.
Clothes and toys, clothes and toys,
I can't wait. I can't wait.

This is Texaco, this is Texaco,
Starts with T, starts with T.
Gas and oil and tune-up, gas and oil and tune-up,
For our car, for our car.

Have students invent their own verses.

4. "When I'm Going Down the Street." This song is sung to the tune "If You're Happy and You Know It":

When I'm going down the street, I see a sign.
When I'm going down the street, I see a sign.
When I'm going down the street, I always think it's neat.
When I'm going down the street, I see a sign.

The stop sign looks just like an octagon.
The stop sign looks just like an octagon.

When I'm going down the street, I always think it's neat.
The stop sign looks just like an octagon.

The yield sign looks just like a triangle.
The yield sign looks just like a triangle.
When I'm going down the street, I always think it's neat.
The yield sign looks just like a triangle.

The railroad sign looks just like a circle.
The railroad sign looks just like a circle.
When I'm going down the street, I always think it's neat.
The railroad sign looks just like a circle.

The billboards look like ugly rectangles.
The billboards look like ugly rectangles.
When I'm going down the street, I always think it's neat.
The billboards look like ugly rectangles.

5. "When I Ride My Bicycle." This song is sung to the tune "Mary Had a Little Lamb":

When I ride my bicycle, bicycle, bicycle,
When I ride my bicycle, I see so many things.

Then have the students name what they see.

I see billboards and stop signs, and stop signs, and stop signs,
I see billboards and stop signs,
I see so many things.

I see Wendy's and Publix, and Publix, and Publix,
I see Wendy's and Publix,
I see so many things.

6. "Old McDonald Went to Town." This song is sung to the tune of "Old McDonald":

Old McDonald went to town,
With a honk-honk, rattle-rattle, crash, beep-beep!
And on his way he saw a stop sign,
With a honk-honk, rattle-rattle, crash, beep-beep!
With a put on the break, put on the break, put on the break!
Old McDonald went to town,
With a honk-honk, rattle-rattle, crash, beep-beep!

You can include the following versus:

And on his way he saw a red light,
With a honk-honk, rattle-rattle, crash, beep-beep!
With a put on the break, put on the break, put on the break!

And on his way he saw a yield sign,
With a honk-honk, rattle-rattle, crash, beep-beep!
With a look to the left, look to the right, look to the left, look to the right!

And on his way he saw a green light,
With a honk-honk, rattle-rattle, crash, beep-beep!
With a keep on going, don't stop, keep on going!

And on his way he saw a dangerous curve sign,
With a honk-honk, rattle-rattle, crash, beep-beep!
With a curve to the right, curve to the left, curve to the right!

And on his way he saw a one-way sign,
With a honk-honk, rattle-rattle, crash, beep-beep!
With a go the right way, not the wrong way!

And on his way he saw a yellow light,
With a honk-honk, rattle-rattle, crash, beep-beep!
With a caution here and a caution there!

And on his way he saw a danger sign,
With a honk-honk, rattle-rattle, crash, beep-beep!
With a look out ahead, look out ahead!

CREATIVE DRAMATICS—"CENTERS" STAGE

 ◆ **SUGGESTED GRADE LEVEL**

PreK–1

 ◆ **PURPOSE/RATIONALE**

◆ Participate in pretend play

 ◆ **MATERIALS**

◆ Props according to unit studied (e.g., napkins and cups from a restaurant, travel brochures from a travel agency)

 ◆ **PROCEDURE**

Create centers, based on units of study or following the children's lead. Allow the children to pretend play using the props and environmental print in the centers. Some centers that promote pretend play and drama include a restaurant center, doctor's office center, travel agency center, grocery store center, and gas station center.

 ◆ **VARIATIONS/EXTENSIONS**

Take a field trip to a business represented by a center in the classroom.

 ◆ **PARENT CONNECTION**

Ask parents to contribute props for the centers.

◆ **ASSESSMENT**

Observe whether children can read and use the environmental print as they play.

◆ **RELATED LITERATURE, SONGS, AND POEMS**

Garfield and the Haunted Diner, by J. Davis
Student-created songs and poems

MUSICAL INSTRUMENT TIME

◆ SUGGESTED GRADE LEVEL

K–2

◆ PURPOSE/RATIONALE

- ◆ Read environmental print
- ◆ Create musical instruments

◆ MATERIALS

- ◆ A variety of containers
- ◆ Tissue rolls
- ◆ Glue and staples
- ◆ Markers
- ◆ Rice, beans, macaroni, bells, and elastic

◆ PROCEDURE

Have available all the materials that could be used to make a musical instrument. Demonstrate a couple of instruments for the children, such as shakers, made from rice and film canisters, and bells attached to elastic. Encourage children to use their imagination as they create their musical instruments. Play a variety of musical recordings in the background as children work.

◆ VARIATIONS/EXTENSIONS

After instruments are made, have the children march or move to music as they use the instruments. A trip to a concert can also be made, or several secondary band students can demonstrate their instruments to the class.

◆ PARENT CONNECTION

Parents can provide materials and help the children make the instruments.

◆ ASSESSMENT

Listen to children as they read the print. Evaluate the children's instruments to determine whether they make a sound.

◆ RELATED LITERATURE, SONGS, AND POEMS

Parade, by D. Crews
The Wheels on the Bus, by P. Zelinsky

CAN YOU MAKE A PUPPET?

◆ SUGGESTED GRADE LEVEL

K-1

◆ PURPOSE/RATIONALE

◆ Create a puppet
◆ Develop oral language skills

◆ MATERIALS

◆ Paper bags
◆ Old socks
◆ Paper plates
◆ Buttons and plastic eyes
◆ Yarn, felt, or pellon
◆ Different textures and types of fabrics
◆ Environmental print material

◆ VARIATIONS/EXTENSIONS

Students are encouraged to invent their own community helper puppet and then answer questions from the class. Questions might include "What is your name? What is your job? How do you help people?"

◆ PARENT CONNECTION

Ask parents to encourage children to think creatively when making their puppets. Parents can also donate materials to the classroom.

◆ ASSESSMENT

Observe children as they read the environmental print. Also, evaluate children's puppets and their responses to the questions of the class.

◆ RELATED LITERATURE, SONGS, AND POEMS

The Milkman, by C. F. Cordsen
Something Good, by R. Munsch
We Keep a Store, by A. Shelby

Print immersion is the key for inventing art, music, and drama related to a unit of study. You, as the teacher, serve as a model for creativity. Can you think of other art, music, and drama activities to introduce to your class?

CHAPTER SEVEN

Meeting the Goals of the National Reading Panel Through Environmental Print Activites

During the past decade, early reading instruction has changed significantly from what and how we taught in the previous century. The Report of the National Reading Panel, *Teaching Children to Read* (2000) defined scientifically based reading instruction. In the introduction to this book, we briefly pointed out two new federal early childhood initiatives designed to implement instruction based on the report from the National Reading Panel. These included Early Reading First, for children ages 3 to 5 years, and Reading First, for children in kindergarten through third grade. Since 2002, Early Reading First and the Reading First initiatives have been integral parts of No Child Left Behind.

Early Reading First programs (for preschool children) emphasize early literacy development through oral language development (vocabulary, expressive language, listening comprehension); phonological awareness (rhyming, blending, segmenting); print awareness; and alphabetic knowledge.

Reading First programs (for children in kindergarten through third grade) emphasize five areas of reading instruction: phonemic awareness, phonics, vocabulary, fluency, and comprehension. We hope you will remember that in Chapter 2 of this book the purposes and rationales for each activity were aligned mainly with Early Reading First goals and a handful of Reading First goals. In this chapter, we make specific suggestions for meeting the goals of Reading First through environmental print activities for children in kindergarten through third grade.

We suggest the following activities for using environmental print to meet the goals of the National Reading Panel:

Phonemic awareness is defined as "the ability to notice, think about, and work with the individual sounds in spoken words. Before children learn to read print, they need to become aware of how the sounds in words work. They must understand that words are made up of speech sounds, or phonemes" (Center for the Improvement of Early Reading Achievement, 2001, p. 2). Since phonemic awareness focuses on sounds, the visual presentation of print may or may not be involved in phonemic awareness games or activities.

Phonemic Awareness Activity: Starts Like . . .

◆ SUGGESTED GRADE LEVEL

K-1

◆ PURPOSE/RATIONALE

◆ Develop phonemic awareness

◆ MATERIALS

◆ List of environmental print words that begin with the same sound (use logos the children have brought to class or words with which they are familiar), for example:

Kmart

Kentucky Fried Chicken

McDonald's

Marshall's

M&M's

Wendy's

Wal-Mart

Walgreen's

◆ PROCEDURE

Ask children to name words that begin with the same sound as an environmental print word. For example, you might say, "I am thinking of a word that begins like the word *Wendy's*. What are some other words that begin like *Wendy's*?"

◆ VARIATIONS/EXTENSIONS

◆ Ask the children to isolate or say the first or last sound in an environmental print word (e.g., "What is the beginning sound of Skittles? What is the ending sound of Skittles?").

◆ Ask the children to blend the separate sounds in a word such as *Jello:* /j/ /e/ /l/ /o/

◆ Ask the students to break words into separate sounds, for example, the word *Velveeta* can be broken into the following sounds: /v/ /e/ /l/ /v/ /e/ /t/ /(schwa)

◆ PARENT CONNECTION

Send a note to parents asking them to point out the beginning sounds of environmental print words at home and in the community as children see the words in context.

◆ ASSESSMENT

Ask the children to name the letter they hear at the beginning of environmental print words currently being used or studied in class.

NOTE: Phonemic awareness activities usually begin with simple words, such as those containing the c/v/c pattern. However, environmental print words are often multisyllabic and irregular.

◆ RELATED LITERATURE, SONGS, AND POEMS

"I Like to Eat Apples and Bananas" (song), by Raffi

PHONICS

Phonics instruction deals with "the relationships between the letters (graphemes) of written language and the individual sounds (phonemes) of spoken language" (Center for the Improvement of Early Reading Achievement, 2001, p. 12). Phonics can be taught in a number of ways. Approaches to phonics instruction include synthetic, analytic, and analogy-based phonics; phonics through spelling; embedded phonics; and onset-rime phonics, just to mention a few. The great thing about environmental print is that it can be used with any of these approaches.

Phonics Activity: Blended Environmental Print

◆ **SUGGESTED GRADE LEVEL**

K-2

◆ **PURPOSE/RATIONALE**

◆ Identify consonant blends

◆ **MATERIALS**

◆ List of environmental print words that begin with consonant blends (use the logos children have brought to class or words with which they are familiar), for example:

Froot Loops

Frosted Flakes

Raisin Bran

Cap'n Crunch

Krystal

Skittles

Rice Krispies

◆ **PROCEDURE**

Ask the students to identify the consonant blend or blends in each logo. Have students think of other words that begin with the same consonant blend—for example, you might ask the children, "What blend do you hear in the first word of *Frosted Flakes?* What blend do you hear in the second word of *Frosted Flakes?* What are some other words that begin with the blend *fr?* What are other words that begin with the blend *fl?*"

PHONICS

◆ VARIATIONS/EXTENSIONS

As children become more proficient with beginning consonant blends, ask them to identify environmental print words that have consonant blends in the ending or medial positions, for example:

Wal-Mart

Kmart

Hardee's

◆ PARENT CONNECTION

Send the list of environmental print words with consonant blends home to parents. Ask parents to say these words slowly to their child and ask the child to identify the consonant blends heard at the beginning (or the end) of the words.

◆ ASSESSMENT

Say the words in the previous lists to children. As you say each word, ask the children to write the two letters they hear at the beginning of each word.

NOTE: Because environmental print helps children relate letters to sounds of words in context, it can be a very effective tool for teaching phonics. Environmental print can also be used as a teacher-made or informal measure of phonics. Informal measures can be made using environmental print words that require phonics through spelling (of these words) or the use of onset-rime phonics.

◆ RELATED LITERATURE, SONGS, AND POEMS

"We Know Our Vowels" is a song sung to the tune of "Bingo":

We know our vowels, yes we do
We know them well, do you?
A-E-I-O-U, A-E-I-O-U, A-E-I-O-U
And sometimes "Y" is added too!

We know the short "a" yes we do
And this is what it says:
"a" as in hat, "a" as in cat, "a" as in sat,
We know it yes we do!

Continue the song with versus for other vowels.

FLUENCY

What exactly is fluency? "Fluency is the ability to read a text accurately and quickly. When fluent readers read silently, they recognize words automatically" (Center for the Improvement of Early Reading Achievement, 2001, p. 22). Researchers have found that fluency helps bridge the gap between word recognition and comprehension.

Fluency Activity: Speedy Shopping List

◆ SUGGESTED GRADE LEVEL

K-3

◆ PURPOSE/RATIONALE

◆ Demonstrate fluency in reading environmental print

◆ MATERIALS

◆ Large collection of environmental print words and logos attached to index cards

◆ PROCEDURE

Ask the students to read the environmental print words as fast as possible.

◆ VARIATIONS/EXTENSIONS

Use flip books, with one word on each page, to keep the index cards from being lost.

Have the students read the environmental print on the walls of the classroom as fast as possible.

Write environmental print words in standard manuscript, or provide the students with a computer-generated list, so they can read the words in manuscript as quickly as possible.

◆ PARENT CONNECTION

Ask parents to share their shopping lists with their child. Encourage parents to model reading each word on the shopping list. Then, have them ask their child to read the shopping list back quickly. To make it a fun game, have the children try to read faster than their parent.

FLUENCY

◆ ASSESSMENT

Fluency activities have a built-in assessment. As students become more proficient at reading, the number of words read per minute should increase. Check the students' ability to read environmental print words quickly and efficiently. Automaticity and ease of reading should be the result of practice.

◆ RELATED LITERATURE, SONGS, AND POEMS

Sing any popular song or folk song that can be sped up as additional verses are added. Make sure children can see the words of the song as they sing it. Fluency in reading requires that students look at the words while reading.

VOCABULARY

How do children learn vocabulary? Most vocabulary is learned indirectly, but some vocabulary must be taught. "Children learn the meanings of most words indirectly, through everyday experiences with oral and written language" (Center for the Improvement of Early Reading Achievement, 2001, p. 35).

Vocabulary Activity: What Goes With This?

◆ **SUGGESTED GRADE LEVEL**

K-2

◆ **PURPOSE/RATIONALE**

- ◆ Categorize environmental print vocabulary

◆ **MATERIALS NEEDED**

- ◆ Environmental print words from the environmental print box

◆ **PROCEDURE**

Ask the students to classify all of the environmental print logos or words. For example, for the word *Hardee's,* you might ask students, "What is this word? The word is *Hardee's.* What is Hardee's? What other words go with Hardee's?"

◆ **VARIATIONS/EXENSIONS**

Have students develop a label for each of their categories:

Fast Food	*Candy*
McDonald's	Skittles
Hardee's	Milky Way
Burger King	M&M's

Have students write the environmental print words in standard manuscript, so they can read the words in manuscript as they classify them. (Remember, students need support in making the transition from logos to standard manuscript.)

VOCABULARY

◆ PARENT CONNECTION

Ask parents to help their child draw a large sketch of the rooms in their home. Have the parents discuss with their child which environmental print items go in each room. Then, have the parents and the children write the names of the products found in each room of the home.

◆ ASSESSMENT

Each student's classification chart or paper can serve as an authentic assessment of the student's ability to classify environmental print vocabulary.

◆ RELATED LITERATURE, SONGS, AND POEMS
Books About Travel, Streets, Signs, and Billboards

Freight Train, by D. Crews

On Market Street, by A. Lobel

Harriet Reads Signs and More Signs, by B. Maestro and G. Maestro

Shopping, Lists, and Stores

General Store, by R. Field

The Cereal Box, by D. McPhail

We Keep a Store, by A. Shelby

Everything from a Nail to a Coffin, by I. Van Rynbach

NOTE: Other related books are listed by classification in Resource A.

COMPREHENSION

"Comprehension is the reason for reading. If readers can read the words but do not understand what they are reading, they are not really reading" (Center for the Improvement of Early Reading Achievement, 2001, p. 48).

Comprehension Activity: Where Do You Find It?

This game is similar to the previous vocabulary activity. However, this activity requires a higher level of understanding and focuses on comprehension. It can be adapted for beginning readers, using pictures, or for more advanced students, using words.

◆ **SUGGESTED GRADE LEVEL**

K-2

◆ **PURPOSE/RATIONALE**

◆ Match the correct logo, picture, or word to its appropriate category

◆ **MATERIALS**

◆ A list of words or pictures to match a set of environmental print logos. Some examples include the following words:

McDonald's (Fast Food)

French fries

Hamburgers

Soft drinks

Food Fair (Grocery Store)

Canned products (with environmental print labels)

Fresh fruit

Ground beef

Soft drinks

Several of the products can be placed in more than one category. Have students discuss their placements to increase comprehension and the students' ability to explain choices.

COMPREHENSION

◆ PROCEDURE

Ask the students to match the correct logo, picture, or word to its appropriate category.

◆ VARIATIONS/EXTENSIONS

For older students, a more specific category of logo could be used to include the product and what the product contains:

Weight Watcher's Lasagna
Ground beef
Pasta
Tomato sauce

◆ PARENT CONNECTION

Send the words and the environmental print logos home and ask the parents to play a game with their child, matching words to the correct environmental print labels. For example, in the category McDonald's, the words *French fries, hamburgers, soft drinks,* and *fast food* would fit.

◆ ASSESSMENT

Authentic comprehension assessment is based on students' charts.

◆ RELATED LITERATURE, SONGS, AND POEMS

General Store, by R. Field
The Little Old Man Who Couldn't Read, by I. S. Black
We Keep a Store, by A. Shelby

Conclusion
Challenges and Opportunities in Using Environmental Print

As you can see, we believe environmental print is a salient tool for teaching children in the early stages of literacy and beyond. Although environmental print is just one piece of the literacy puzzle, it is a very important one. As with any large jigsaw puzzle, when one piece is missing, the puzzle is incomplete.

Environmental print instruction is not without its challenges and possibilities. Though we could discuss many challenges and possibilities, we see two that can make a difference in the lives of children and world in which we all live: reflective teaching and transformational teaching.

 ## Reflective Teaching

Environmental print must be taught by reflective practitioners. Although teaching for some has become a technician's job, with teacher-proof materials and scripted programs, good teachers have to make ethical decisions about how and what to teach children. With this in mind, some people have criticized environmental print as promoting inappropriate consumerism and mindless commercialism. Others are critical of businesses that want to sponsor schools with their own brand of environmental print. These critics state, "Our schools are not for sale." We agree.

Teachers using environmental print must take these ideas into consideration. We are grateful to Yetta Goodman, who carefully reviewed this book and suggested that teachers must always have a legitimate purpose for using environmental print and be able to communicate this purpose to their students and their students' families. To do so, teachers must be reflective practitioners, always considering appropriate and legitimate uses of environmental print while simultaneously considering the challenge environmental print poses in terms of consumerism and commercialism. (For more information on teachers as reflective decision makers, see Bredekamp & Copple, 1997.)

Transformational Teaching

There are many ways to talk about teaching. We have found one of the easiest and most helpful is to consider teaching as transmission, transaction, or transformation (Aldridge & Goldman, 2002; Jungck & Marshall, 1992). Simply put, transmission is similar to direct instruction in that the teacher transmits information to the students. Transaction involves active learning, in which students choose from several activities prepared by the teacher. Finally, transformation is teaching with the goal of making a difference in the world. So what does this have to do with environmental print? The answer has to do with what we see as a wonderful challenge and possibility when teaching with environmental print.

Just as being a reflective practitioner is necessary when using environmental print, teaching to make a difference is also a remarkable possibility. Many of the activities in this book involve transmission. Transmission is necessary for teaching social knowledge. Even the smartest children in the world cannot learn the alphabet without some form of transmission. Some activities in this book were designed around transaction. Activities that provide children with simple choices were designed for transactional teaching. These are necessary to learning, too. However, the biggest challenge is using environmental print, or any material, to make a difference in the world.

When we were completing this book, one of our finest students (Kelly Russell), who uses environmental print, was surprised when we told her we wanted to share ideas for using environmental print to make a difference in the world. She wondered, "How can this be? How can it be done?" Here are a few short examples.

When Lynn taught kindergarten, a stuffed bear belonging to her class went missing. The students decided to use environmental print to make "Lost" posters to be distributed throughout the school. This resulted in the students finding the bear in a neighboring kindergarten class. Then Lynn encouraged her students to develop a lost and found center in her classroom so that the students could help others. Always thinking of ways to turn teaching, including environmental print instruction, into a transformational experience, Lynn encouraged her students to clean up the playground and discuss the environmental print packages found on the playground.

While transmission and transaction activities seem to occur naturally with environmental print instruction, transformation sometimes has to be jump-started. We encourage you to be not only a reflective practitioner but also a transformational teacher—always looking for ways to teach with environmental print to make a difference in the world. We wish you well on that journey!

Resource A
Environmental Print Book List

General

Black, I. S. (1965). *The little old man who couldn't read.* Chicago: Whitman.

Cutting, B., & Cutting, J. (1988). *Reading is everywhere.* San Diego, CA: Wright Group.

Frandsen, K. G. (1984). *I started school today.* Chicago: Children's Press.

Grainger, J. (1983). *Matthew likes to read.* Wellington, NZ: School Branch.

Hood, S. (2000). *Look! I can read!* New York: Scholastic.

Stanek, M. (1986). *My mom can't read.* Chicago: Whitman.

Travel, Streets, Signs, and Billboards

Arnold, T. (1992). *The signmaker's assistant.* New York: Dial Books.

Arthur, M. (1993). *Arthur's family vacation.* Boston: Little, Brown.

Bloom, S. (2001). *The bus for us.* Honesdale, PA: Boyds Mills Press.

Cole, J. (1987). *The magic school bus inside the earth.* New York: Scholastic.

Cole, J. (1989). *The magic school bus inside the human body.* New York: Scholastic.

Cole, J. (1990). *The magic school bus lost in the solar system.* New York: Scholastic.

Cordsen, C. F. (2005). *The milkman.* New York: Dutton Children's Books.

Crews, D. (1978). *Freight train.* New York: Scholastic.

Crews, D. (1980). *Truck.* New York: Greenwillow.

Crews, D. (1981). *Light.* New York: Greenwillow.

Crews, D. (1983). *Parade.* New York: Greenwillow.

Crews, D. (1984). *School bus.* New York: Greenwillow.

Cuyler, M. (2000). *Roadsigns: A harey race with a tortoise.* New York: Winslow Press.

Davis, J. (1978). *Garfield and the haunted diner.* New York: Grossett & Dunlap.

Ellis, S. (2000). *Next stop!* Toronto: Fitzhenry & Whiteside.

Hill, M. (2003). *Signs at the park.* New York: Children's Press.

Hill, M. (2003). *Signs at the store.* New York: Children's Press.

Hill, M. (2003). *Signs on the road.* New York: Children's Press.

Hoban, T. (1983). *I can read signs.* New York: Greenwillow.

Hoban, T. (1983). *I can read symbols.* New York: Greenwillow.

Hutchins, P. (1980). *The tale of Thomas Mead.* New York: Greenwillow.

Keats, E. J. (1972). *Pet show.* New York: Macmillan.

Khalsa, D. K. (1988). *My family vacation.* New York: Potter.

Klove, L. (1996). *I see a sign.* New York: Simon & Schuster.

Lobel, A. (1981). *On market street.* New York: Greenwillow.

Maestro, B., & Maestro, G. (1981). *Harriet reads signs and more signs.* New York: Crown.

Maestro, B., & Maestro, G. (1989). *Taxi.* New York: Houghton Mifflin.

Milich, Z. (2002). *City signs.* Toronto, Canada: Kids Can Press.

Thomas, I. (1976). *My street's a morning cool street.* New York: Harper & Row.

Van Laan, N. (1992). *People, people, everywhere!* New York: Knopf.

Zelinsky, P. (1990). *The wheels on the bus.* New York: Dutton Children's Books.

Zion, G. (1957). *Dear garbage man.* New York: Harper & Row.

Recipes and Cooking

Bastyra, J. (1997). *Pizza fun.* New York: Kingfisher Chambers.

Campbell Soup Company. (2004). *Campbell kids alphabet soup.* New York: Harry N. Abrams.

dePaola, T. (1978). *Pancakes for breakfast.* New York: Harcourt, Brace, Jovanovich.

Erlbach, A. (1994). *Peanut butter.* Minneapolis: Lerner.

Kasza, K. (1987). *The wolf's chicken stew.* New York: Putnam.

Katzen, M., & Henderson, A. (1994). *Pretend soup and other recipes.* Berkeley, CA: Tricycle Press.

Kovalski, M. (1990). *Pizza for breakfast.* New York: Morrow Junior Books.

Low, A. (1993). *The popcorn shop.* New York: Scholastic.

McGrath, B. B. (1994). *The M&M's counting book.* Watertown, MA: Charlesbridge.

Pallotta, J. (1999). *The Hershey's Milk Chocolate Bar fractions book.* New York: Cartwheel Books.

Riley, L. (1997). *Mouse mess.* New York: Scholastic.

Schuette, S. L. (2003). *An alphabet salad: Fruits and vegetables from A to Z.* Mankato, MN: Capstone.

Sendak, M. (1970). *In the night kitchen.* New York: Harper & Row.

Steig, W. (1998). *Pete's a pizza.* New York: HarperCollins.

Stevens, J. (1999). *Cook-a-doodle-doo!* New York: Harcourt, Brace.

Sturges, P. (1999). *The little red hen (makes a pizza).* New York: Scholastic.

Wellington, M. (2004). *Crepes by Suzette.* New York: Dutton.

Westcott, N. B. (1987). *Peanut butter and jelly.* New York: Penguin.

Zemach, M. (2005). *Eating up Gladys.* New York: Scholastic.

Shopping Lists and Stores

Berenstain, S., & Berenstain, J. (1985). *The Berenstain bears and too much junk food.* New York: Random House.

Berenstain, S., & Berenstain, J. (1988). *The Berenstain bears get the gimmies.* New York: Random House.

Field, R. (1988). *General store.* New York: Scholastic.

Fryer, G. (1986). *Supermarket.* Tokyo: Froebel-kan.

Gretz, S. (1982). *Teddy bears go shopping.* New York: Four Winds.

Hill, M. (2003). *Signs at the store.* New York: Children's Press.

Hutchins, P. (1976). *Don't forget the bacon.* New York: Greenwillow.

Maestro, B. (1993). *The story of money.* New York: Clarion Books.

McPhail, D. (1974). *The cereal box.* Boston: Little, Brown.

Munsch, R. (1990). *Something good.* Toronto, Canada: Annick.

Shelby, A. (1990). *We keep a store.* New York: Orchard.

Van Rynbach, I. (1991). *Everything from a nail to a coffin.* New York: Orchard Books.

Restaurants and Menus

Axelrod, A. (1994). *Pigs will be pigs.* New York: Four Winds Press.

Davis, J. (1978). *Garfield and the haunted diner.* New York: Grossett & Dunlap.

Letters and Notes

Ahlberg, J., & Ahlberg, A. (1986). *The jolly postman.* Boston: Little, Brown.

Ahlberg, J., & Ahlberg, A. (1991). *The jolly Christmas postman.* Boston: Little, Brown.

Keats, E. J. (1968). *A letter to Amy.* New York: Harper & Row.

Leedy, L. (1991). *Messages in the mailbox*. New York: Holiday House.
Mayer, M. (1987). *There's an alligator under my bed*. New York: Dial.
Sherman, A. (1964). *Hello Mudduh, hello Fadduh!* New York: Harper & Row.
Shulevitz, U. (1990). *Toddlecreek post office*. New York: Farrar, Straus, and Giroux.
Weiss, L. (1984). *My teacher sleeps in school*. New York: Frederick Warne.

Gardening

Anno, M. (1992). *Anno's magic seeds*. New York: Philomel.
Cole, H. (1995). *Jack's garden*. New York: Greenwillow.
Pallotta, J. (1994). *The spice alphabet book*. Watertown, MA: Charlesbridge.
Pattou, E. (2001). *Mrs. Spitzer's garden*. New York: Harcourt.
Robbins, K. (2005). *Seeds*. New York: Atheneum.
Saksie, J. (1995). *The seed song*. Cypress, CA: Creative Teaching Press.
Wellington, M. (2005). *Zinnia's flower garden*. New York: Dutton Children's Books.

Weather

dePaola, T. (1975). *The cloud book*. New York: Scholastic.

Environment

Showers, P. (1994). *Where does the garbage go?* New York: HarperCollins.

Related Literature

Axelrod, A. (1997). *Pigs will be pigs*. New York: Aladdin.
Ehlert, L. (1993). *Eating the alphabet*. New York: Harcourt Children's Books.
Falwell, C. (1995). *Feast for ten*. New York: Clarion Books.
Hutchings, R. (1997). *The gummy candy counting book*. New York: Scholastic.
Leedy, L. (1997). *Measuring Penny*. New York: Henry Holt.
McMillan, B. (1991). *Eating fractions*. New York: Scholastic.
McMillan, B. (1996). *Jelly beans for sale*. New York: Scholastic.
Pallotta, J. (1998). *Reese's Pieces peanut butter: Counting board book*. New York: Corporate Board Books.
Sweeney, J. (2002). *Me and the measure of things*. New York: Random House.
Trisler, A. (1989). *Words I use when I write*. Cambridge, MA: Modern Learning Press.
Williams, R. L. (1995). *We can make graphs*. Huntington Beach, CA: Creative Teaching Press.
Williams, R. L. (2001). *The coin counting book*. Watertown, MA: Charlesbridge Publishing.

*A few books on this list are older classics and may be out of print but still available in your school library.

Resource B
Sample Letter to Parents

Dear Parents,

One of the strategies a child must develop for reading is print awareness. One way to encourage this development is through the use of environmental print, which includes any print not found in books. Environmental print is print available to children in their environment. Most children come to school with a broad base of familiar print known as environmental print, including logos and labels found in grocery stores, such as Tide, Crest, and Heinz; billboards, such as McDonald's, Burger King, Taco Bell; and last, functional print, such as stop signs, speed limit signs, and so on.

Please take the time to point out this print to your child when you shop or drive around our community. Also, the print they read, such as labels from cans or napkins and containers from fast-food restaurants, are valuable tools for learning. Please allow your child to bring this print to school often to share with our class. I have an area that is set aside for environmental print, but the success of the center depends on your child and you. The research we have completed in our kindergarten has shown how this type of print enhances print awareness.

Please keep in mind that environmental print is only one strategy I use to encourage young readers. It is, however, a good way to begin to show children how meaningful and functional print is in a familiar context. Along with the alphabet center, environmental print also aids in relating symbols with phonetic sounds, another strategy for reading.

Please do not hesitate to call me if you have any questions. Thank you for your help.

Sincerely,

Carta de la maestra a los padres

Queridos padres:

Una de las estrategias que su niño debe desarrollar es elreconocimiento de la escritura. Una forma para animar este progreso es el uso de la lectura ambiental. Esta incluye cualquier escritura no encontrada en libros. Es la literatura disponible para el niño en su ambiente. La mayoría de los pequeños vienen a la escuela familiarizados ampliamente con la lectura conocida como lectura ambiental. Encierra las insignias y las etiquetas halladas en las tiendas o mercados tales como Tide, Crest, Heinz, etc., avisos o carteleras tales como McDonalds, Burger King, Taco Bell, etc. y finalmente lectura funcional, como por ejemplo, las señales de las paradas, las advertencias de los límites de velocidad, etc.

Por favor, tómese su tiempo para enseñarle al niño la lectura ambiental cuando usted hace compras o conduce alrededor de la comunidad. También, la interpretación que hacen al leer, por ejemplo, en las etiquetas de las latas, servilletas o los envases de restaurantes de comida rápida, que son valiosas herramientas para este aprendizaje. Permita, por favor, que su menor traiga a la escuela a menudo este tipo de escritura, para incorporarla como parte de nuestra clase. Yo tengo un área del salón donde pongo la escritura ambiental, pero el éxito de ese centro depende de su niño y de usted. La investigación que hemos hecho en nuestro jardín de infancia ha demostrado cómo este tipo de actividad realza el conocimiento de la lecto-escritura.

Tenga, por favor, presente que la lectura ambiental es solamente una estrategia que utilizamos a fin de animar a los niños a leer. Es, sin embargo, una buena manera para comenzar a demostrar a los pequeños cómo la lectura es significativa y funcional cuando está en un contexto familiar. Junto con el centro de lectura, la literatura ambiental también se relaciona con los símbolos de los sonidos fonéticos, otra estrategia para la lectura.

No vacile, así mismo, en llamarme si usted tiene cualquiera pregunta. Gracias por su ayuda.

Firma

References

Adams, M. J. (1990). *Beginning to read: Thinking and learning about print.* Cambridge, MA: MIT Press.

Aldridge, J., & Goldman, R. (2002). *Current issues and trends in education.* Boston: Allyn & Bacon.

Aldridge, J., & Rust, D. (1987). A beginning reading strategy. *Academic Therapy, 22*(3), 323-326.

Bissex, G. L. (1980). *Gnys at wrk: A child learns to write and read.* Cambridge, MA: Harvard University Press.

Bredekamp, S., & Copple, C. (Eds.). (1997). *Developmentally appropriate practice in early childhood programs* (Rev. ed.). Washington, DC: National Association for the Education of Young Children.

Bronfenbrenner, U. (1977). Toward an experimental ecology of human development. *American Psychologist, 32,* 513-531.

Bronfenbrenner, U. (1986). Ecology of the family as a context for human development: Research perspectives. *Development Psychology, 22*(6), 723-742.

Center for the Improvement of Early Reading Achievement. (2001). *Putting reading first: The research building blocks for teaching children to read.* Bethesda, MD: National Institute of Child Health and Human Development.

Christie, J. F., Enz, B. J., Gerard, M., & Prior, J. (2002, May). *Using environmental print as teaching materials and assessment tools.* Paper presented at the 47th annual convention of the International Reading Association, San Francisco.

Clay, M. (1993). *An observation survey of early literacy achievement.* Portsmouth, NH: Heinemann.

Cloer, T., Aldridge, J., & Dean, R. (1981/1982). Examining different levels of print awareness. *Journal of Language Experience, 4*(1&2), 25-33.

Copple, C., & Bredekamp, S. (2005). *Basics of developmentally appropriate practice: An introduction to teachers of children 3 to 6.* Washington, DC: National Association for the Education of Young Children.

Cromwell, L., & Hibner, D. (1976). *Finger frolics.* Livonia, MI: Partner Press.

Cummins, C. (Ed.). (2006). *Understanding and implementing Reading First initiatives: The changing role of administrators.* Newark, DE: International Reading Association.

Disney. (1977). *Disney children's favorites, Vol. 2* [CD]. Los Angeles: Author.

Enz, B. (2006). Phonemic awareness: Activities that make sounds come alive. In C. Cummins (Ed.), *Understanding and implementing Reading First initiatives: The changing role of administrators* (pp. 23-36). Newark, DE: International Reading Association.

Feldgus, E., & Cardonick, I. (1999). *Kid writing.* Bothell, WA: Wright Group.

Ferreiro, E., & Teberosky, A. (1982). *Literacy before schooling* (K. Castro, Trans.). Portsmouth, NH: Heinemann.

Fountas, I. C., & Pinnell, G. S. (1996). *Guided reading: Good first teaching for all children.* Portsmouth, NH: Heinemann.

Goodman, Y. (1980). The roots of literacy. In M. P. Douglass (Ed.), *Claremont Reading Conference: Forty-fourth yearbook* (pp. 1-32). Claremont, CA: Claremont Reading Conference, Center for Developmental Studies.

Goodman, Y. (1984a). Children coming to know literacy. In W. H. Teale & E. Sulzby (Eds.), *Emergent literacy: Writing and reading* (pp. 1-14). Norwood, NJ: Ablex.

Goodman, Y. (1984b). *The developmental initial literacy.* In H. Goelman, A. Oberg, & E. Smith (Eds.), *Awakening to literacy* (pp. 102-109). Portsmouth, NH: Heinemann.

Goodman, Y. (Ed.). (1986). *How children construct literacy.* Newark, DE: International Reading Association.

Goretta, C. (Producer). (1977). *Piaget on Piaget: The epistemology of Jean Piaget* [Motion picture]. New Haven, CT: Yale University Media Design Studios.

Harste, J., Burke, C., & Woodward, V. (1982). Children's language and world: Initial encounters with print. In J. A. Langer & M. T. Smith-Burke (Eds.), *Reader meets author—Bridging the gap: A psycholinguistic and sociolinguistic perspective* (pp. 105-131). Newark, DE: International Reading Association.

Jungck, S., & Marshall, J. D. (1992). Curricular perspectives on one great debate. In S. Kessler & B. B. Swaderner (Eds.), *Reconceptualizing the early childhood curriculum: Beginning the dialogue.* New York: Teachers College Press.

Kamii, C. (1991). What is constructivism? In C. Kamii, M. Manning, & G. Manning (Eds.), *Early literacy: A constructivist foundation for whole language* (pp. 17-29). Washington, DC: National Education Association.

Kirkland, L., Aldridge, J., & Kuby, P. (1991). Environmental print and the kindergarten classroom. *Reading Improvement, 28,* 219-222.

Kuby, P., & Aldridge, J. (1997). Direct versus indirect environmental print instruction and early reading ability in kindergarten children. *Reading Psychology: An International Quarterly, 18,* 91-104.

Kuby, P., Aldridge, J., & Snyder, S. (1994). Developmental progression of environmental print recognition in kindergarten children. *Reading Psychology: An International Quarterly, 15,* 1-9.

Kuby, P., Goodstadt-Killoran, I., Aldridge, J., & Kirkland, L. (1999). A review of research on environmental print. *Journal of Instructional Psychology, 26*(3), 173-183.

Laminack, L. (1991). *Learning with Zachary.* Richmond Hill, Ontario, Canada: Ashton Scholastic.

Lee, L. (1989). *Emergent literacy in Chinese: Print awareness of young children in Taiwan.* Unpublished doctoral dissertation, University of Arizona, Tempe.

Letchman, H., Finn, D., & Aldridge, J. (1991). Environmental print as strategy for developmental literacy of young atypical children. *Perceptual and Motor Skills, 73,* 413-414.

McCracken, R., & McCracken, M. (1986). *Stories, songs, and poetry to teach reading and writing.* Winnipeg, Canada: Peguis Publishers.

McGee, L. (1986). Young children's environmental print reading. *Childhood Education, 63,* 118-125.

Miller, L. (1996). *Towards reading: Literacy development in the preschool years.* Milton Keynes, UK: Open University Press.

Miller, L. (1998). Literacy interactions through environmental print. In R. Campbell (Ed.), *Facilitating preschool literacy* (pp. 100-118). Newark, DE: International Reading Association.

National Institute of Child Health and Human Development. (2000). *Report of the National Reading Panel: Teaching children to read: An evidence-based assessment of the scientific research literature on reading and its implications for reading instruction* (NIH Publication No. 00-4769). Washington, DC: U.S. Government Printing Office.

National Reading Panel. (2000). *Report of the National Reading Panel: Teaching children to read.* Bethesda, MD: National Institute of Child Health and Human Development.

Neuman, S., & Roskos, K. (1993). Access to print for children of poverty: Differential effects of adult mediation and literacy enriched play settings on environmental print and functional print tasks. *American Educational Research Journal, 30,* 95-122.

No Child Left Behind Act of 2001, Pub. L. No. 107-110,115 Stat. 1425 (2003).

Piaget, J. (1970). *Science of education and the psychology of the child* (D. Coltman, Trans.). New York: Penguin.

Piper, T. (2003). *Language and learning: The home and school years* (3rd ed.). Upper Saddle River, NJ: Merrill.

Prior, J., & Gerard, M. R. (2004). *Environmental print in the classroom: Meaningful connections for learning to read.* Newark, DE: International Reading Association.

Schickedanz, J. (1986). *More than ABC's.* Washington, DC: National Association for the Education of Young Children.

Shapiro, E., & Mitchell, A. (1992). Principles of the Bank Street Approach. In A. Mitchell & J. David (Eds.), *Explorations with young children: A curriculum guide from the Bank Street College of Education* (pp. 15-22). Mt. Rainier, MD: Gryphon House.

U.S. Department of Education. (2002). *Early reading first.* Retrieved March 26, 2006, from http://www.ed.gov/programs/earlyreading/index.html

Vukelich, C. (1994). Effect of play interventions of young children's reading of environmental print. *Early Childhood Research Quarterly, 9,* 153-170.

Vygotsky, L. (1978). *Interactions between learning and development.* In M. Cole, V. John-Steiner, S. Scribner, & E. Souberman (Eds.), *Mind in society* (pp. 79-91). Cambridge, MA: Harvard University Press.

Wepner, S. (1985). Linking logos with print for beginning reading success. *Reading Teacher, 38,* 633-639.

Woodward, V., Harste, J., & Burke, C. (1984). *Language stories and literacy lessons.* Portsmouth, NH: Heinemann.

Ylisto, I. (1967). *An empirical investigation of early reading responses of young children.* Unpublished doctoral dissertation, University of Michigan, Ann Arbor.

CORWIN PRESS

The Corwin Press logo—a raven striding across an open book—represents the union of courage and learning. Corwin Press is committed to improving education for all learners by publishing books and other professional development resources for those serving the field of PreK–12 education. By providing practical, hands-on materials, Corwin Press continues to carry out the promise of its motto: **"Helping Educators Do Their Work Better."**